I0017665

DATA ANALYTICS WITH MS EXCEL & POWER BI

This book will transform you into Data Analytics Expert . In this Book you will learn how to use MS Excel and Power Bi to read, clean, transform, visualize and analyze the data.

Punit Prabhu

Copyright © 2021 Punit Prabhu

All rights reserved

The characters and events portrayed in this book are fictitious. Any similarity to real persons, living or dead, is coincidental and not intended by the author.

No part of this book may be reproduced, or stored in a retrieval system, or transmitted in any form or by any means, electronic, mechanical, photocopying, recording, or otherwise, without express written permission of the publisher.

CONTENTS

INTRODUCTION TO DATA ANALYTICS

What is Data Analytics?

Data Analytics is the process of exploring and analyzing large data sets to help data driven decision making.

Analyze Data

Decision Making

Definition

Data when suitably filtered and analysed along with other related Data
Sources and a suitable Analytics applied can provide valu-

able information to various organizations, industries, business, etc. in

the form of prediction, recommendation, decision and the like.

Applications of Data Analytics

Finance & Accounting, Business analytics, Fraud , Healthcare, Information Technology, Insurance, Taxation , Internal Audit, Digital forensic, Transportation, Food, Delivery, FMCG, Planning of cities, Expenditure, Risk management, Risk detection, Security, Travelling, Managing Energy, Internet searching, Digital advertisement , etc.

Real life examples of Data Analytics

1. Coca-Cola

Coca Cola uses big data analytics to drive customer retention.

In the year 2015, Coca-Cola managed to strengthen its data strategy by building a digital-led loyalty program. According to a Forbes article, Coca Cola was one of the first globally recognized brands, outside of the tech sector, to embrace Big Data. In 2015, for example, they were able to determine that Coca Cola products were mentioned online once every two seconds. Having access to this information helps them understand who their customers are, where they live, and what prompts them to discuss the brand.

2. Netflix

Netflix is a good example of a big brand that uses big data analytics for tar-

geted advertising. With over 100 million subscribers, the company collects huge data, which is the key to achieving the industry status.If you are a subscriber, you are familiar to how they send you suggestions of the next movie you should watch. Basically, this is done using your past search and watch data. This data is used to give them insights on what interests the subscriber most. See the screenshot below showing how Netflix gathers big data.

3. UOB Bank

UOB bank from Singapore is an example of a brand that uses big data to drive risk management. Being a financial institution, there is huge potential for incurring losses if risk management is not well thought of. UOB bank recently tested a risk management system that is based on big data. The big data risk management system enables the bank to reduce the calculation time of the value at risk. Initially, it took about 18 hours, but with the risk management system that uses big data, it only takes a few minutes. Through this initiative, the bank will possibly be able to carry out real-time risk analysis in the near future.

4. Amazon Fresh and Whole Foods

Amazon leverages big data analytics to move into a large market. The data-driven logistics gives Amazon the required expertise to enable creation and achievement of greater value. Focusing on big data analytics, Amazon whole foods is able to understand how customers buy groceries and how suppliers interact with the grocer. This data gives insights whenever there is need to implement further changes.

5. Pepsico

PepsiCo is a consumer packaged goods company that relies on huge volumes of data for an efficient supply chain management. The company is committed to ensuring they replenish the retailers' shelves with appropriate volumes and types of products. The company's clients provide reports that include their warehouse inventory and the POS inventory to the company, and this data is used to reconcile and forecast the production and shipment needs. This way, the company ensures retailers have the right products, in the right volumes and at the right time. Listen to this webinar where the company's Customer Supply Chain Analyst talks about the importance of big data analytics in PepsiCo Supply chain.

Data Analytics with Excel and Power BI

Excel and Power Bi are powerful, flexible tools for every analytics activity. Both can be used to get broad data analytics and visualization capabilities. We can easily gather, shape, analyze, and explore key business data in new ways—all in less time—using both apps together.

Data analytics in Excel and Power is done by Importing the data from various sources and linking it with excel and power bi, cleaning and transform the data, manipulate and analyze the data using visuals.

Introduction of Software to be used in the course

1. MS Office Tools – Excel, Word, Power Point

A. Microsoft Excel

Basics of Excel

There are 5 important areas in the screen.

1. **Quick Access Toolbar:** This is a place where all the important tools can be placed. When you start Excel for the very first time, it has only 3 icons (Save, Undo, Redo). But you can add any feature of Excel to to Quick Access Toolbar so that you can easily access it from anywhere (hence the name).

2. **Ribbon:** Ribbon is like an expanded menu. It depicts all the features of Excel in easy to understand form. Since Excel has 1000s of features, they are grouped in to several ribbons. The most important ribbons are – Home, Insert, Formulas, Page Layout & Data.

3. **Formula Bar:** This is where any calculations or formulas you write will appear. You will understand the relevance of it once you start building formulas.

4. **Spreadsheet Grid:** This is where all your numbers, data, charts & drawings will go. Each Excel file can contain several sheets. But the spreadsheet grid shows few rows & columns of active spreadsheet. To see more rows or columns you can use the scroll bars to the left or at bottom. If you want to access other sheets, just click on the sheet name (or use the shortcut CTRL+Page Up or CTRL+Page Down).

5. **Status bar:** This tells us what is going on with Excel at any time. You can tell if Excel is busy calculating a formula, creating a pivot report or recording a macro by just looking at the status bar. The status bar also shows quick summaries of selected cells (count, sum, average, minimum or maximum values). You can change this by right clicking on it and choosing which summaries to show.

Excel Options

General:- The most commonly used settings, such as user interface settings, default font for new workbooks, number of sheets in a new workbook, customer name, and Start screen.

Formulas:- All options for controlling calculation, error-checking rules, and formula settings. Note that options for multithreaded calculations are currently considered obscure enough to be on the Advanced tab rather than on the Formulas tab.

Proofing:- Spell-check options and a link to the AutoCorrect dialog.

Save:- The default method for saving, AutoRecovery settings, legacy colours, and web server options.

Language:- Choose the editing language, ToolTip language, and Help language.

Advanced:- All options that Microsoft considers arcane, spread among 13 headings.

Customize Ribbon:- Icons to customize the ribbon.

Quick Access Toolbar:- Icons to customize the Quick Access Toolbar (QAT).

Add-Ins:- A list of available and installed add-ins. New add-ins can be installed from the button at the bottom of this category.

Trust Center:- Links to the Microsoft Trust Center, with 12 additional categories.

2. Installation of Power Query, Power Pivot and Data Analysis tool pack Addins in Excel

For MS office versions 2016 and above Power Query, Power Pivot are by default installed in Excel. Power query is in Data Tab. Power Pivot add in needs to be enabled from Developer Tab → Com Add ins. Data Analysis Tool pack add in can be enabled from Developer Tab → Excel Add ins.
For MS office version 2013 Power Query needs to be installed by downloading the add in from below link
https://www.microsoft.com/en-in/download/details.aspx?id=39379

BASICS & NAVIGATION

Excel is a software program created by Microsoft that uses spreadsheets to organize numbers and data with formulas and functions. Excel analysis is ubiquitous around the world and used by businesses of all sizes to perform financial analysis.

Excel makes it easy to crunch numbers. With Excel, you can streamline data entry. Then, get chart recommendations based on your data, and create them with one click. Or, easily spot trends and patterns with data bars, color coding, and icons

1. **Excel Interface**

    I.   First time when you open MS Excel below is the window you will see

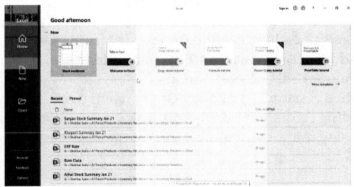

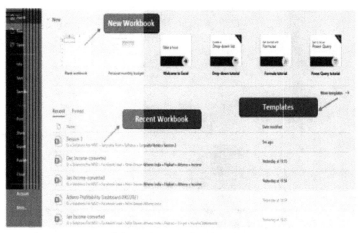

- Open New workbook by clicking on Blank workbook
- Recent – Open workbook which you have worked in past

- Templates – There are various standard templates provided which can be used for various purposes instead of preparing a report //from scratch. As shown in Below Image

II. File Tab

- Info – Protect Workbook & Properties. With Protect workbook, a sheet or workbook can be protected with password, workbook can be made read only, Restrict access like to edit, copy or print, Mark the file as final.

- Properties – Gives information about the Excel file like size, author, last modified, created on and etc.

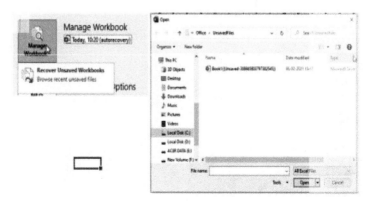

- Manage Workbook- Recover unsaved workbook as shown in the image

- Save and Save As – Save option saves in current location. Save As – Change file name, Location, change file type.
- Print – Print selected print area in workbook and sheet
- Share – Share it on onedrive
- Export – PDF, Change file type as shown in Image

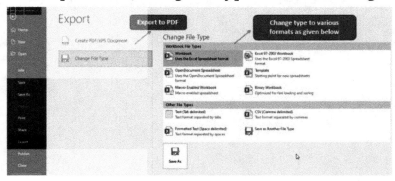

- Publish – Save it in onedrive and publish it on Power Bi
- Account – Update Excel and About as shown in Image

III. Home Tab

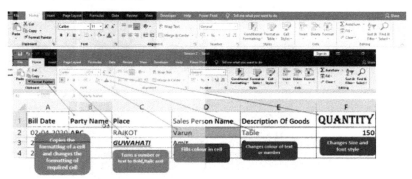

- Clipboard – Paste, Cut, Copy and Format painter
- Font – Change fonts and font type, color, size and borders

- Alignment – Alignment of text or numbers in excel. Left, Right, center, middle, Merge and wrap

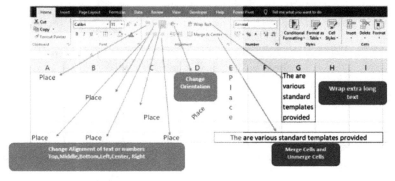

- Number – Change type of text and numbers

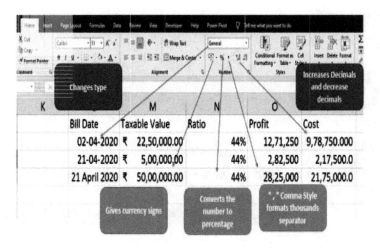

- Styles – Conditional Formatting, Format as Table, Cell Styles

Conditional formatting is used to format cells depending on the need. Various formatting rules are available in the tab. In current image duplicate values are highlighted.

Format As Table is used to format a data in table and give various themes as shown in Image

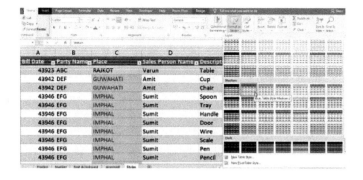

Cell Styles feature is used to change cell styles depending on the input to be highlighted

In below image calculated cells are highlighted.

- Cells – Insert, Delete and Format

With Insert feature you can insert cells, rows, columns and sheet.

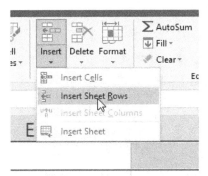

on Of Goods | Quantit

With Delete feature you can delete cells, rows, columns and sheet.

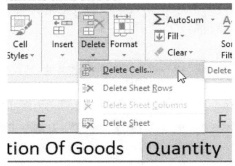

tion Of Goods | Quantity

With Format feature you can change height of Rows, Autofit row height, Hide or unhide rows & columns, Organize sheets, and protection of sheet, lock cell and format cells

- Editing – Autosum, Fill, Clear, Sort and filter, Find

and Select

Clear feature – Clears formatting, comments, hyper-links as shown below

Sort & Filter – Put filter on selected data range, Sorts the data largest to smallest and vise versa, clears filter.

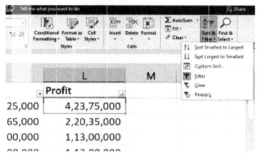

Find & Select feature – Used to find certain data, re-place , go to a page/line/cell, Find   formulas ,comments, formatting, contents, select objects .

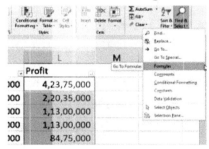

Autosum – Apply formulas with just click of a button with this feature.

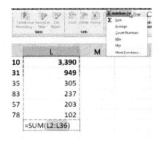

	L	M
10	3,390	
31	949	
35	305	
83	237	
57	203	
78	102	
	=SUM(L2:L36)	

IV. Insert Tab

- Tables

Converts a normal range of data in Table

After converting the data range into Table. Design tab is enabled. With this feature you can change name of table, resize table, create pivot, remove duplicates, convert again to normal range, insert slicers, change styles and change the theme of table.

Insert slicer – Click on insert slicer to slice and dice

the data according to various categories in data. It works as a filter (Detailed explanation will be given in Pivot table and slicer chapter

Pivot – Arrange and summarize complex data. Click on Pivot table and select range. Select New worksheet or Existing worksheet. A Pivot table is created, select data from Pivot table fields and plot the data in pivot table as shown below.

(Detailed explanation will be given in Pivot table & Slicer Topic)

Recommended Pivot – Customized set of pivot tables derived from Data. With this feature you can select required pivots instead of creating it from scratch.

- Illustrations – Used to insert pictures, Shapes, Smart Art and screenshot

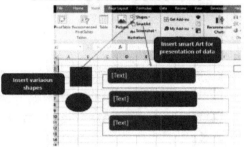

- Add-ins – Use pre installed add ins for visualizing data or install new add ins.

Charts ,Tours & Sparklines – Insert charts to visualize the data (Detailed explanation will be given in Charts topic)

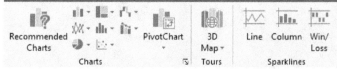

- Filters – Slicer feature Same as shown above
- Links – Insert hyperlink

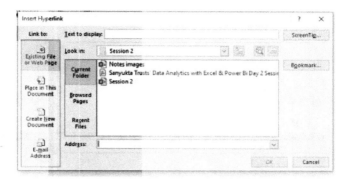

- Text – Insert Text box, header & Footer , Word Art, Signature line and Object as shown in image.

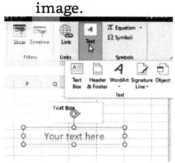

- Symbols – Add symbols and mathematical equation

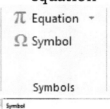

V. Page Layout

- Themes – Change theme, colors, font and effects of objets of entire workbook at just one click.

- Page setup & Scale to fit options are used for printing the document.
- Arrange

Bring object forward or send object backward.

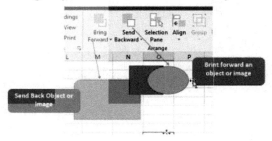

Align – Align objects as per options given

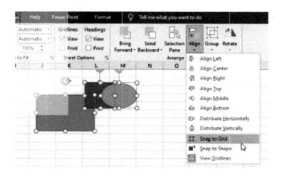

Group objects together or ungroup .

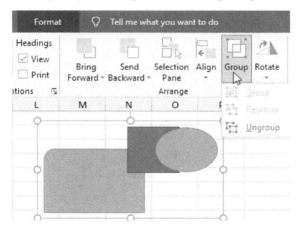

VI. Formulas

- Functions library – contains various formulas and functions to be covered in Formula chapter
- Defined names – Define cell with name and use them in formulas.

Trace precedents and Trace Dependents – Show arrows that indicate which value affect the selected cell, Evaluate – Evaluate a formula step by step

- Calculations – Perform automatic or manual calculation of formulas

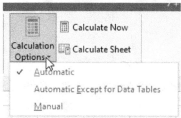

VII. Data

- Get and Transform Data – Power Query Addin Detailed explanation in Power query chanpter
- Connections - Detailed explanation in Power query chanpter
- Sort & Filter – Sorts Data Ascending and descending order

- Data Tools - Detailed explanation in formatting and Power pivot chapter
- Forecast – Detailed explanation in Formulas chapter
- Outline – Detailed explanation in Formatting chapter

VIII. Review

- Proofing –

Workbook statistics gives details as shown in image

- Accessibility – Checks if file follows accessibility best practices
- Insights – Gives insights of data selected from web
- Language – Translate selected text into desired language
- Comments – Insert comments, Delete and show comments
- Protect - Protect sheet , workbook and allow Edit ranges with password.

IX. View

- Workbook views

Normal – See document in normal view

Page breakup preview – to see where page breaks before printing

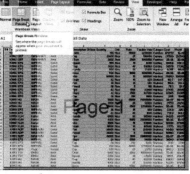

- Show

Gridlines – Show or Remove gridlines

Formula bar – Show or Remove formula bar

Headings – Show or remove headings

As shown in image there are no gridlines , formula bar and headings.

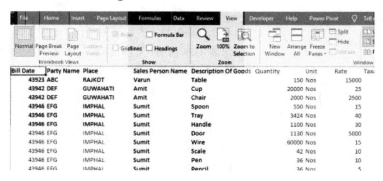

- Zoom – Zoom in and out in the sheet
- Window

Freeze Panes – Freeze Row or column , Free row and column together to keep visible headers or column freezed while u scroll the document

X. Developer

- Code – Visual basic is macro editor, Macros gives list of macros, Record macros records commands you perform while recording, Use relative reference macros are recorded with actions relative to initial selected cell cell
- Add-ins – With Addin you can add new addins from web and Microsoft store,

Excel add in manage available addins, Comm Addins manage available addins

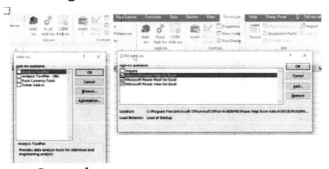

- Controls –

Insert contains form and active x controls

Properties – View of modify properties of selected control

View code – View macro codes

- XML – Manage XML

XI. Help

- Help
- Community

XII.   Tell me what you want to do

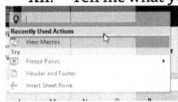

This feature is available from MS 16 version. In this feature you can search excel related functions.

XIII.   Status Bar

- Page features

- Sheet features

- Sheet tab Features

FORMULAS & FUNCTIONS

1. Formulas

A formula is an expression that operates on value in a range of cell or cells.

Data			Ans	Formula
20	50	10	3	=+(C2-B2)/D2

2. Functions

Functions are predefined formulas in excel which eliminate manual entry of formulas while give them names.

B	C	D
	Data	
20	50	10
Ans	Formula	
80	=SUM(B2:D2)	

Five Ways to Insert Formula in Excel

1. Typing formula inside the cell

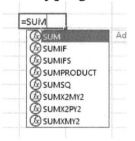

2. Using Insert Function in Formulas Tab

3. Selecting Formulas from one of groups in Formula Tab

4. Using AutoSum

5. Recently Used from Formula Tab

FUNCTIONS

There are more than 470 functions in Excel and there are additions addin functions also with help of VBA macros you can create your own formula.

Functions are distributed in Below Categories:- Financial, Logical, Text, Date & Time, Lookup & Reference, Math & Trig, More Functions.

We don't need to learn all formulas. I have listed down some important formulas which are used in analysis.

1. Financial Formulas

1. NPV – Calculates the net present value of cash flows based on a discount rate

Syntax = NPV(rate,value1,value2…)

Arguments –

1. Rate is rate of discount over the length of period
2. Value1 is cashflow value. Only number value is considered rest all is ignored

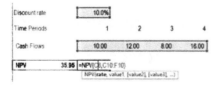

Discount rate	10.0%			
Time Periods	1	2	3	4
Cash Flows	10.00	12.00	8.00	16.00
NPV	35.95	=NPV(C8,C10:F10)		

NPV(rate, value1, [value2], [value3], ...)

2. XNPV – calculates the NPV of cash flows based on a discount rate and specific dates

Syntax = XNPV(rate,values,dates)

1. Rate = Discount rate for a period
2. Values = Positive or negative cash flows (an array of values)

3. Dates = Specific dates (an array of dates)

Discount rate	10.0%			
Initial Investment	5,000			
Returns	01-01-2017	03-01-2018	03-01-2019	03-01-2020
Cash Flows	10.00	12.00	8.00	16.00

XNPV	39.53	=XNPV(C16,C19:F19,C18:F18)
		XNPV(rate, values, dates)

3. IRR – this formula calculates the internal rate of return (discount rate that sets the NPV to zero)

Syntax = IRR(values,[guess]

Values - Positive or negative cash flows (an array of values)

Guess - An assumption of what you think IRR should be

Guess	0.20				
Returns	Initial Investn	01-01-2017	03-01-2018	03-01-2019	03-01-2020
Cash Flows	-20	10.00	12.00	8.00	16.00

IRR	0.41	=IRR(C32:G32,C30)
		IRR(values, [guess])

4. XIRR – calculates the internal rate of return (discount rate that sets the NPV to zero) with specified dates

Syntax = XIRR(values,dates,guess)

Guess	0.20				
Returns	Initial Investn	01-01-2017	03-01-2018	03-01-2019	03-01-2020
Cash Flows		(20.00)	12.00	8.00	16.00

XIRR	0.34	=XIRR(D39:G39,D38:G38,C37)
		XIRR(values, dates, [guess])

5. SLN – calculates depreciation based on the straight-line method

Syntax = SLN(cost,salvage,life)

Cost – cost of asset when bought

Salvage – Value of asset after depreciation

Life – Number of period for which asset is depreciated

Cost	100000
Salvage Value	25000
Years	10

SLN	7,500.00	=SLN(C24,C25,C26)
		SLN(cost, salvage, life)

2. Logical Formulas

1. AND - It is used to determine if the given conditions in a test are TRUE

Syntax = AND(logical1,logical2...)

2. False - Returns the logical value FALSE

Syntax = FALSE()

3. IF - Specifies a logical test to perform

Syntax = IF(Logical_test,[value_if_true],[value_if_false])

4. IFERROR - Returns a value you specify if a formula evaluates to an error; otherwise, returns the result of the formula. It can be used with other formulas to handle errors.

Syntax = IFERROR(value,value_if_error)

5. IFNA - Returns the value you specify if the expression resolves to #N/A, otherwise returns the result of the expression

Syntax = IFNA(value,value_if_na)

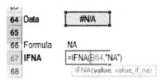

6. NOT - Reverses the logic of its argument
Syntax = NOT()

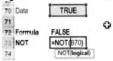

7. OR - Returns TRUE if any argument is TRUE, If neither condition is met, then it returns FALSE
Syntax = OR(logical1,logical2..)

8. TRUE - Returns the logical value TRUE
Syntax = TRUE()

9. XOR - Returns a logical exclusive OR of all arguments. With XOR the return is TRUE if the number of true arguments is odd.
Syntax = XOR(logical1,logical2..)

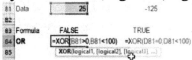

3. Text Formulas

1. Left - Returns the left most characters from a text value.
Syntax = LEFT(text,num_chars)

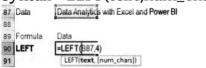

2. Right - Returns the last character or characters in a text string, based on the number of bytes you specify
Syntax = RIGHT(text,num_chars)

3. Mid - Returns a specific number of characters from a string starting at a specified position

Syntax = MID(text,start_num,num_chars)

4. Proper - Capitalizes the first letter in each word of a text value

Syntax = PROPER(text)

5. Upper - Converts text to uppercase

Syntax = UPPER(text)

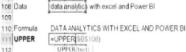

6. Lower - Converts text to lowercase

Syntax = LOWER(text)

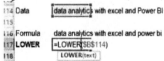

7. LEN - Returns the number of characters in a text string

Syntax = LEN(text)

8. Trim - Removes all spaces from text except single spaces between words

Syntax = TRIM(text)

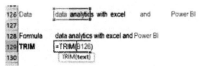

9. Substitute - Substitutes new text for old text in a text string

Syntax = SUBSTITUTE(text,old_text,new_text,instance_num)

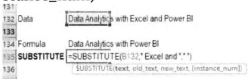

10. Concatenate – Joins text in various cells

Syntax = CONCATENATE(text,text2...)

4. Date & Time Formulas

1. Year - Converts an Excel date / time serial number to a year

Syntax = YEAR(serial_number)

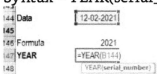

2. Month - The formula returns the month number in the year of the date represented by the date / time serial number.

Syntax = MONTH(serial_number)

3. Today - The TODAY function returns the current date according to the computer's system clock.

Syntax = TODAY()

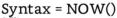

156	Formula	12-02-2021
157	**TODAY**	=TODAY()
158		TODAY()

4. Now – Returns the Excel date / time serial number of the current date and time. Volatile.

Syntax = NOW()

159	Formula	12-02-2021 19:06
160	**TODAY**	=NOW()
161		NOW()

5. Hour, Minute, Second

162	Time	19:10:05
163	HOUR	19 =HOUR(B162)
164	MINUTE	10 =MINUTE(B162)
165	SECOND	5 =SECOND(B162)

6. NETWORKDAYS - The Excel Networkdays function calculates the number of work days between two supplied dates (including the start and end date). The calculation includes all weekdays (Mon - Fri), excluding a supplied list of holidays.

Syntax = NETWORKDAYS(start_date,end_date,holi-days)

167	Data	01-02-2021	28-02-2021
168	NETWORKDAYS	20	
169	Formula	=NETWORKDAYS(B167,C167)	
170		NETWORKDAYS(start_date, end_date, [holidays])	

7. EOMONTH - The Excel Eomonth function returns the last day of the month, that is a specified number of months before or after an initial supplied start date.

Syntax = EOMONTH(start_date,months)

170		
171	Data	01-02-2021
172	EOMONTH	31-12-2021
173	Formula	=EOMONTH(B171,10)
174		EOMONTH(**start_date**, months)

5. Lookup & Reference Formulas
    1. MATCH - Returns the relative position of an item in an array that matches a specified value in a specified order. Important mainly as a feeder to other lookup functions because it returns the position of an item in a range.

Syntax = MATCH(lookup_value,lookup_array,match_type)

    2. INDEX - An unusual function that takes alternative forms depending upon whether the first argument is an array or a reference. It is one of the most valuable functions for extracting data from tables whether as individual items, entire rows, or columns. It is used with other functions especially with MATCH.

Syntax = INDEX(array,row_num,column_num)
             =   INDEX(reference,row_num,column_num,area_num)

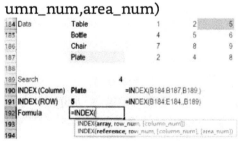

    3. OFFSET - Returns a reference to a range that is a specified number of rows and columns from a cell or range of cells. Often used with calculated row and column numbers to return a cell or range address.

Syntax = OFFSET(reference,rows,cols,[height],[width])

4. VLOOKUP - Looks in the first column of an array and moves across the row to return the value of a cell

Syntax = VLOOKUP(lookup_value,table_array_index_num,range_lookup)

= range_lookup has 2 options TRUE for approx. match and FALSE for exact match

5. HLOOKUP - Looks in the top row of a table or array and returns the value of the indicated cell.

Syntax = HLOOKUP(lookup_value,table_array_index_num,range_lookup)

6. ROW & COLUMN – Gives row and column number reference

7. HYPERLINK – Creates hyperlink

8. INDIRECT - Returns a reference indicated by a value provided as text.

6. Statistical, INFO & Math functions

231	Data	100	
232		500	
233			
234		600	
235			
236	SUM	1200	=SUM(B231:B234)
237	Average	400	=AVERAGE(B231:B234)
238	SUBTOTAL	1200	=SUBTOTAL(9,B231:B234)
239	COUNT	3	=COUNT(B231:B234)
240	COUNTA	3	=COUNTA(B231:B234)
241	COUNTBLANK	1	=COUNTBLANK(B231:B234)
242	ISBLANK	TRUE	

1. SUM – Adds all numbers in range of cell
2. Average – Returns average i.e arithmetic mean of arguments
3. COUNT – Counts number of cells in range that contain numbers
4. COUNTA – Counts number of cell in a range that are not empty
5. COUNTBLANK – Counts number of blank cells
6. ISBLANK – If a cell value is blank it will give output as TRUE

7. MAX & MIN

MAX = Gives max number in a range
MIN = Gives min number in a range

244	Data	100	
245		500	
246		600	
247			
248	MIN	100	=MIN(B244:B246)
249	MAX	600	=MAX(B244:B246)

8. SUMIF

Syntax = SUMIF(range,criteria,sum_range)

9. Product – Multiplies all arguments
Syntax = PRODUCT(number1,number2...)

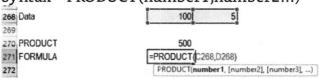

10. Round, Roundup, Rounddown – Round decimal numbers

FORMATTING

Spreadsheets are often seen as boring and pure tools of utility, but that doesn't mean that we can't bring some style and formatting to our spreadsheets

Formatting helps your user find meaning in the spreadsheet without going through each and every individual cell. Cells with formatting will draw the viewer's attention to the important cells.

In Excel, formatting worksheet data is easy. You can use several fast and simple ways to create professional-looking worksheets that display your data effectively. For example, you can use document themes for a uniform look throughout all of your Excel spreadsheets, styles to apply predefined formats, and other manual formatting features to highlight important data.

Formatting a Data

Raw Data

Row Labels	Sales	Cost	Profit	Profit Ratio
Anjar	1604043596	583582054.8	1020461541	0.636180677
BHUJ	4207865654	1376250299	2831615356	0.672933879
GUWAHATI	3984474760	1406588941	2577885819	0.646982595
IMPHAL	33730671594	10545515110	23185156484	0.687361247
Karnal	8815143082	2810530510	6004612572	0.681170177
NAGAON	5575483131	1729065260	3846417871	0.68988064
NASIK	13047294371	4345659644	8701627727	0.66692967
RAJKOT	2101724398	653041412.2	1448682986	0.689283042
Grand Total	73066700586	23450240230	49616460356	0.67905708

Using Font, Number tabs as shown in image to do a simple formatting

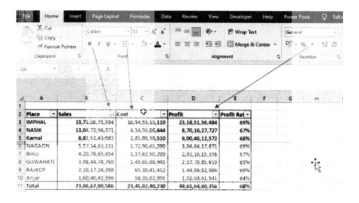

Formatting a Data with help of formatting tools in Excel

As shown in image , we have Product category wise data with Taxable value, Cost, Profit and Profit Ratio.

There are no gridlines, headers, formula bar and ribbon, these can be hidden with formatting tools.

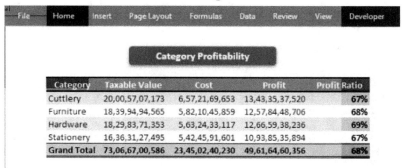

Category	Taxable Value	Cost	Profit	Profit Ratio
Cuttlery	20,00,57,07,173	6,57,21,69,653	13,43,35,37,520	67%
Furniture	18,39,94,94,565	5,82,10,45,859	12,57,84,48,706	68%
Hardware	18,29,83,71,353	5,63,24,33,117	12,66,59,38,236	69%
Stationery	16,36,31,27,495	5,42,45,91,601	10,93,85,35,894	67%
Grand Total	73,06,67,00,586	23,45,02,40,230	49,61,64,60,356	68%

In Below Image you can see Formula tab,

header and grid-lines

In Below image there is none. Untick grid-lines, headings and formula bar.

Below is a Report prepared using various formatting tools like chart and Smart Art.

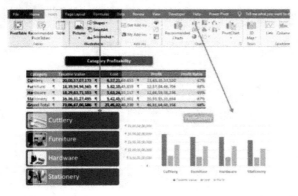

As shown above we can convert a simple data into a nice and presentable form with the help of formatting tools available in Excel.

As shown in image below, with this style of formatting and presenting a data there is no need to rework the data and show it in PowerPoint.

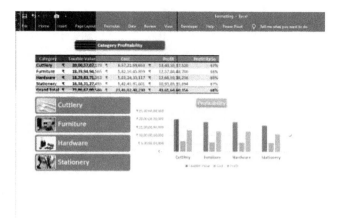

Types of Formatting

Press Ctrl +1 or

1. Numeric

I. Date formatting

II. Special Formatting – Change Security code number formatting and Phone number formatting.

III. Custom Formatting
You can custom a formatting as required

2. Display
In Home Tab – Font feature
Change font of the text , size, Colour
Fill colours in cell
Apply borders
Underline, Bold or Italic a character

	A	B	C	D	E
1	2021 Budget Projections				
2		Jan	Feb	Mar	1st Q
3	Gross Revenue				
4	Sales	₹ 1,01,000.00	₹ 1,38,370.00	₹ 1,39,750.00	₹ 3,79,120.00
5	Shipping	₹ 18,700.00	₹ 26,970.00	₹ 30,240.00	₹ 75,910.00
6	Gross Revenue	₹ 1,19,700.00	₹ 1,65,340.00	₹ 1,69,990.00	₹ 4,55,030.00

3. Tools
Justify option allows the text copied from internet or word to be changed.

Background – Change background from Page layout option

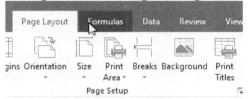

4. Row & Column
Data with no Row or column formatting

	A	B	C	D	E	F
1	Employee Name	Department	Hire Date	Benefits	Salary	Job Rating
2	Aguilar, Kevin	Environmental Health/S	12-15-86	R	#####	1
3	Chase, Troy	Operations	10-22-01		#####	3
4	Chavez, Thomas	Logistics	2-23-89	DMR	#####	3
5	Pruitt, Randy	Manufacturing	4-30-01	DM	#####	1
6	Potter, Dawn	Professional Training Gr	7-12-87	DMR	#####	4

After adjusting row and column

	A	B	C	D	E	F
1	Employee Name	Department	Hire Date	Benefits	Salary	Job Rating
2	Aguilar, Kevin	Environmental Health/Safety	12-15-86	R	69,060	1
3	Chase, Troy	Operations	10-22-01		57,520	3
4	Chavez, Thomas	Logistics	2-23-89	DMR	64,510	3
5	Pruitt, Randy	Manufacturing	4-30-01	DM	70,760	1
6	Potter, Dawn	Professional Training Group	7-12-87	DMR	87,950	4
7	Dominguez, Duane	Manufacturing	4-3-04	M	71,490	5
8	Andrews, Diane	Quality Assurance	12-8-89	DMR	54,200	4
9	Hess, Brian	Admin Training	1-22-88	DM	30,445	1

5. Outlining
Data Tab – Outline -- Subtotal

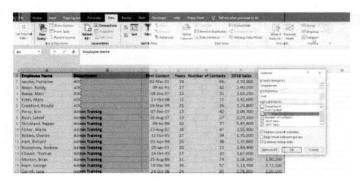

After Outline

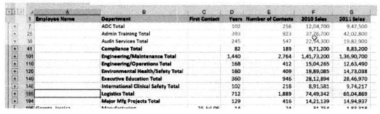

		Employee Name	Department	First Contact	Years	Number of Contacts	2010 Sales	2011 Sales
+	7		ADC Total		102	256	12,04,700	9,47,500
+	28		Admin Training Total		393	923	37,26,700	42,02,800
+	30		Audit Services Total		245	547	22,94,300	19,82,900
+	41		Compliance Total		82	189	9,71,200	8,83,200
+	101		Engineering/Maintenance Total		1,440	2,764	1,41,73,200	1,36,90,700
+	110		Engineering/Operations Total		168	412	15,04,265	12,63,490
+	120		Environmental Health/Safety Total		160	409	19,89,085	14,73,038
+	140		Executive Education Total		360	946	28,12,894	28,46,970
+	148		International Clinical Safety Total		102	218	8,91,581	9,74,217
+	186		Logistics Total		712	1,889	74,49,342	65,04,869
+	194		Major Mfg Projects Total		129	416	14,21,139	14,94,937
	196	Goorie, Jessica	Manufacturing	25 Jul 06	14	24	31,754	1,82,318

Grouping

Data Tab – Outline -- Group

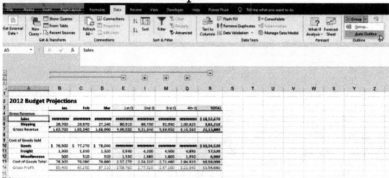

6. Visualization

Sparklines – Insert High, Low, first, last, negative markers.

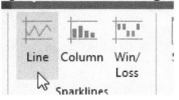

Line Column Win/
                Loss

Sparklines

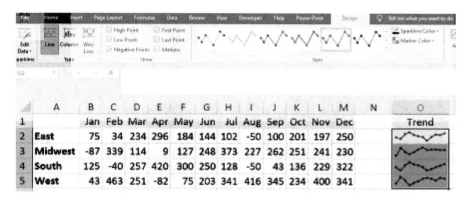

	Jan	Feb	Mar	Apr	May	Jun	Jul	Aug	Sep	Oct	Nov	Dec	Trend
East	75	34	234	296	184	144	102	-50	100	201	197	250	
Midwest	-87	339	114	9	127	248	373	227	262	251	241	230	
South	125	-40	257	420	300	250	128	-50	43	136	229	322	
West	43	463	251	-82	75	203	341	416	345	234	400	341	

WordArt

Shape Effects

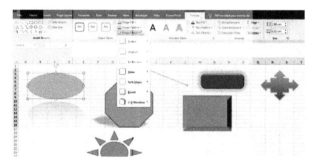

Themes
Pagelayout – Colours or Themes

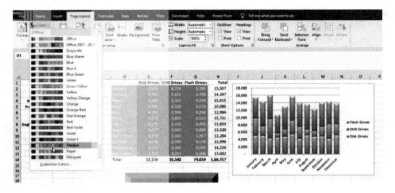

7. Conditional

Home – Conditional Formatting – there are various options for formatting as shown in image.

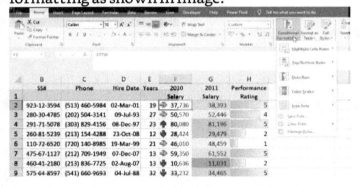

Conditional Formatting with Formula

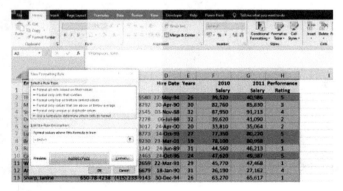

PIVOT TABLE & SLICER

A PivotTable is a powerful tool to calculate, summarize, and analyze data that lets you see comparisons, patterns, and trends in your data.

Create a Pivot Table

1. Select data you want to create PivotTable from
2. Select > Insert PivotTable

3. Under Choose the data that you want to analyze, select Select a table or range.

4. In Table/Range, verify the cell range.

5. Under Choose where you want the PivotTable report to be placed, select New worksheet to place the Pivot-Table in a new worksheet or Existing worksheet and then select the location you want the PivotTable to appear.

6. Select OK.

7. Drag fields

The PivotTable Fields pane appears. To get the total quantity of each product, drag the following fields to the different areas.

1. Place field to the Rows area.

2. Quantity field to the Values area.

3. Sales Person field to the Filters area.

8. Sort

To get Imphal at the top of the list, sort the pivot table.

Click any cell inside the Sum of Quantity column.

Right click and click on Sort, Sort Largest to Smallest.

9. Change Summary Calculation

By default pivot summarizes or counts the data. But it can be changed. There 3 ways which are as follows

1. Click any cell inside the Sum of Quantity column.
2. Right click and click on Value Field Settings.

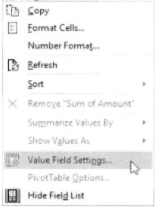

3. Choose the type of calculation you want to use. For example, click Count.

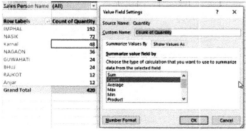

10. Show Values As

1. Normal % to Grand Total -- Change the calculation by show values as. In current example its % Grand

Total.

Insert Quantity Column 2nd time and perform the step if you want to see both the Value and Percentage.

2. % of Parent Row Total

Select Category and put in Rows. Place will be Parent.
Select % of Parent row total for % of Category in each Place.

3. % Different From and Rank

% Different from – Calculate % difference from Previous, Next or any particular month.

Rank calculation – Rank Largest to smallest and smallest to largest.

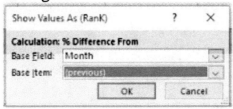

11. Two Dimensional Pivot with drill down

Tow Dimensional – Party name in columns and Date series in rows.

Drill down – Year , Quarter, Month in rows can be drilled up from month to quarter to year by clicking on ⊞ and ⊟(signs

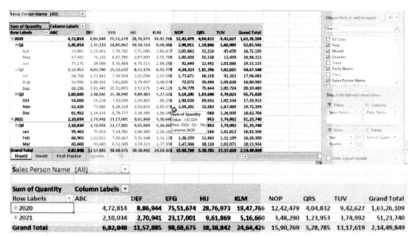

Sum of Quantity	Column Labels								
Row Labels	ABC	DEF	EFG	HIJ	KLM	NOP	QRS	TUV	Grand Total
+ 2020		4,72,814	8,86,944	75,51,674	28,76,973	19,47,766	12,42,479	4,04,832	9,42,627	1,63,26,109
+ 2021		2,10,034	2,70,941	23,17,001	9,61,869	5,16,660	3,48,290	1,23,953	3,74,992	51,23,740
Grand Total		6,82,848	11,57,885	98,68,675	38,38,842	24,64,426	15,90,769	5,28,785	13,17,619	2,14,49,849

Also you can right click and select Expand or Colapse

12. Defer layout update

In Defer layout update you can select the required fields and then update

This feature is used for huge data which takes time for updating.

13. Calculated Fields

Create a formula in Pivot table with the help of calculated fields.

As percentage cannot be summarized in pivot. It would show wrong answer hence with the help of calculate field you can calculate percentages and also other formulas

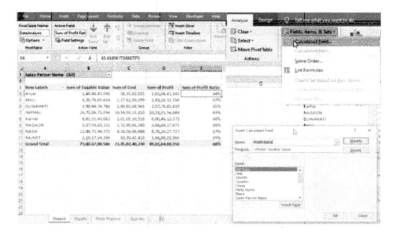

14. Move the field

15. Filter

Because we added the Sales Person field to the Filters area, we can filter this pivot table by Sales Person.

1. Click the filter drop-down and select any sales person.

16. Design Tab

1. Report Layout – Change the layout of pivot to tabular and other options

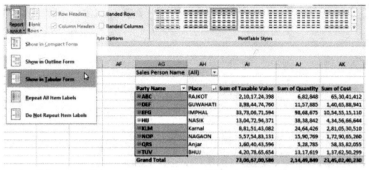

2. Pivot table styles , Grand Total and sub total
Change the style of pivot from pivot table styles
Turn on or off Grand total or subtotals

17. Show Filter pages
Change name of Pivot table in Pivot table name
Show report filter pages and create separate pages for each
sales person in filter.

Slicers

1. Click on Insert slicer in Analyze tab and choose the fields

2. Create multiple Pivots and control them with slicers

Right click on the slicer and click on Report connections and choose the pivots you want to control with slicers.

3. Design Tab for Slicers

In Buttons and size field change the number of columns, heights, width of buttons and size of slicer in size feature. Arrange the slicers in arrange feature. Change styles of slicer and also you can create new styles for slicer

4. Slicer settings

Click on slicer setting in Design tab the below dialogue box will open

Change name , Sort , Hide items with no data, Show items with no data are some settings which can be done.

5. Slicers can be used to filter pivots in whole workbook but the pivots should be from same data source.
6. With Slicer you can control pivots, slice and dice the data very easily
7. Slicer selection

Select any field to filter the data and click on clear filter to remove selection.

With multi select feature besides filter icon you can select multiple fields or you can use Press Ctrl and then select with mouse.

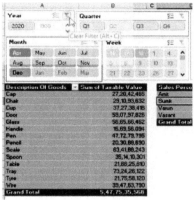

POWER QUERY

What is Power Query

Power Query is a data transformation and data preparation engine. Power Query comes with a graphical interface for getting data from sources and a Power Query Editor for applying transformations. Because the engine is available in many products and services, the destination where the data will be stored depends on where Power Query was used. Using Power Query, you can perform the extract, transform, and load (ETL) processing of data.

How Power Query helps with data acquisition

Business users spend most of their time on data preparation, which delays the work of analysis and decision-making. Several challenges contribute to this situation, and Power Query helps address many of them.

Existing challenge	How does Power Query help?
Finding and connecting to data is too difficult	Power Query enables connectivity to a wide range of data sources, including data of all sizes and shapes
Experiences for data connectivity are too fragmented	Consistency of experience, and parity of query capabilities over all data sources
Data often needs to be re-shaped before consumption	Highly interactive and intuitive experience for rapidly and iteratively building queries over any data source, of any size

Any shaping is one-off and not repeatable	When using Power Query to access and transform data, you define a repeatable process (query) that can be easily refreshed in the future to get up-to-date data. In the event that you need to modify the process or query to account for underlying data or schema changes, you can use the same interactive and intuitive experience you used when you initially defined the query.
Volume (data sizes), velocity (rate of change), and variety (breadth of data sources and data shapes)	Power Query offers the ability to work against a subset of the entire dataset to define the required data transformations, allowing you to easily filter down and transform your data to a manageable size. Power Query queries can be refreshed manually or by taking advantage of scheduled refresh capabilities in specific products (such as Power BI) or even programmatically (by using the Excel object model). Because Power Query provides connectivity to hundreds of data sources and over 350 different types of data transformations for each of these sources, you can work with

	data from any source and in any shape.

Power Query experiences

The Power Query user experience is provided through the Power Query Editor user interface. The goal of this interface is to help you apply the transformations you need simply by interacting with a user-friendly set of ribbons, menus, buttons, and other interactive components.

The Power Query Editor is the primary data preparation experience, where you can connect to a wide range of data sources and apply hundreds of different data transformations by previewing data and selecting transformations from the UI. These data transformation capabilities are common across all data sources, whatever the underlying data source limitations.

When you create a new transformation step by interacting with the components of the Power Query interface, Power Query automatically creates the M code required to do the transformation so you don't need to write any code.

Transformations

The transformation engine in Power Query includes many pre-built transformation functions that can be used through the graphical interface of the Power Query Editor. These transformations can be as simple as removing a column or filtering rows, or as common as using the first row as a table header. There are also advanced transformation options such as merge, append, group by, pivot, and unpivot.

All these transformations are made possible by choosing the transformation option in the menu, and then applying the options required for that transformation. The following illustration shows a few of the transformations available in Power Query Editor.

Image showing the transformation commands under the Transform, Home, and Add Column tabs of the Power Query Editor

Get & Transform

Click on Data Tab → Inn Get and Transform → From Table
For 2013 its under Power Query Tab

After clicking on From Table Power Query Editor will open as shown in Image

In Power Query Editor you can clean and transform the data.

After Importing Sales Data. Go to Home tab in Power query Editor and click on Close and Load To

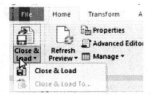

Load to window will appear. Click on Only create connection and click on Load.

Now Import Location Master from master sheet in assignment file into power query

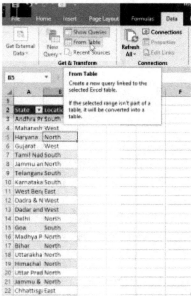

Click Data Tab →Select a cell in a table →Click From Table

For Excel 2013 – Power query tab → Select a cell in a table → Click From Table

Create a Reference Query from Sales Data. Right Click on the Sales

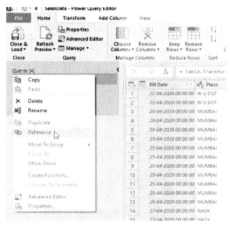

Reference Query creates a Copy of the Query with previous steps stored in Sales Data.
Whatever steps performed in original query are reflected in Reference query.

Change the name of the query as "Sales Analysis"

Next we will merge Location data with Sales data and insert new column of Location with the help of common column "State". Click on Merge Queries in Home tab → Merge Queries.

A merge window will appear. Select "State" column from Sales Analysis in 1st table. In 2nd table select Location data → Select "State" column. In Join Kind select "Left Outer" and Click **OK**.

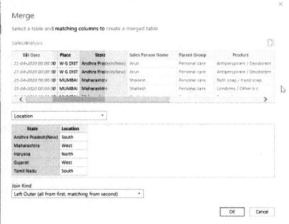

A new column gets inserted name "Location". Click on the double arrows to expand the column.

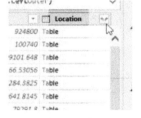

Select "Location" and untick on "Use Original Column name prefix". Click Ok . "Location" Column will be inserted.

Next Step Change the type of Bill Date column and convert it to "Date" format.

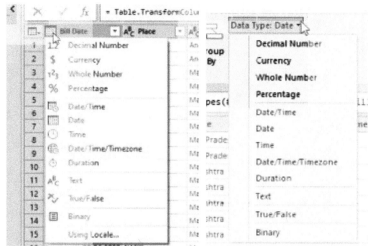

There are 2 ways to change the Format type.

1) In Home tab → click on Data Type → change the format from selection

2) Top left corner of Column click on the icon and change the format type.

Insert Year Column – Select the Bill Date column. Go to Add Column Tab → Column from examples → From Selection

A New column will be inserted. Type "Year" select the year. Press Enter and Click OK

Same way Insert Month Column. Select Bill Date Column again, Go to Add column select column from examples then Frpm selection. In New Column Type "Month" press enter and click Ok Insert Day column following above steps.

Insert **Profit Ratio** Column. Go to Add column tab. Select Custom column. A Custom column window appears. Type Profit Ratio in New Column Name. In Custom column formula Select the Column heading "Profit" press "/" and select "Sales Value" click on "Ok". Same way Insert **Cost Ratio**

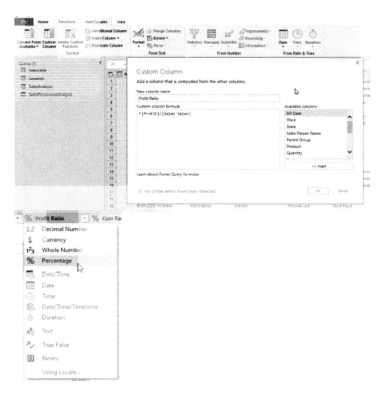

Change type to Percentage

Create a Reference Query of Sales Analysis from Queries Tab.
Name it as Sales Person Analysis.

Se-
lect Sales Person Name, Quantity, Sales Value, Cost, Profit, Year, Month Name, Cost Ratio.

Now Group By the Columns. Select the Sales Person Name and click on Group by. Group By feature summarizes the data.

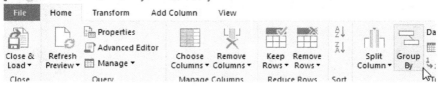

In Group by Select "Advanced". One part Select only Text columns. In 2nd part select number and value columns. In Operation select "Sum" Select Column Quantity, Sales Value and Profit and click OK. To add more column click on Add aggrega-

tion.

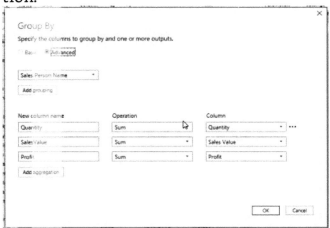

Create Profit % Column. Go to Add column tab → Custom Column. In the Custom window select Profit the press "/" and the select Sales Value and press OK

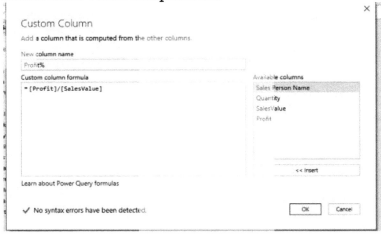

Change the type to Percentage.

GO to Home tab → Close and Load To. Select "Table" and click Ok

A new table is created in Excel for Sales Person Analysis.

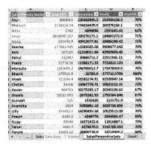

Workbook Queries Tab. This tab stores All the Queries created in the Excel file. You can anytime Edit queries as required by double clicking on any query or Right click and edit.

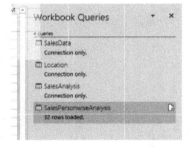

Right click on the query . You will get various options to edit queries.

Importing Excel file from a "Folder"

Save the data shared of Sales Data – CY and PY in a folder and name it as Sales.

Open a blank Excel workbook and Save it as Sales Analysis Report.

Click on Data Tab → New Query → From File → From Folder

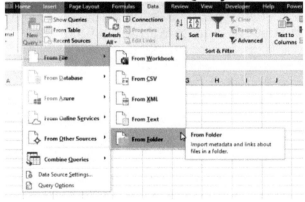

Next a new dialog box will appear as shown in image. Click on Browse and select the folder you want to import. Import the "CY" Folder. After locating the folder click on "CY" and Click on Open.

Click on OK and let it load.

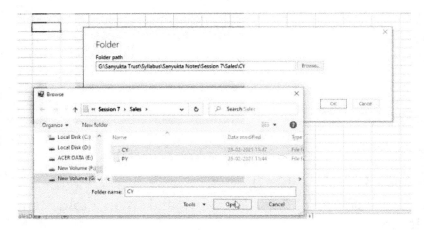

A new window will pop up. Click on Combine and Load To

In Combine files window Select the relevant sheet. In current file select "Sheet1" and click "OK"

Click on "Only create connection"

Follow Similar steps and import "PY" Folder.

After Importing both the folders the query is stored and can be seen in workbook queries pane.

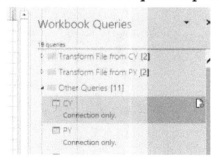

To access power query editor double click on the queries or

Right click and click on Edit.

Append Queries

Now Append both CY and PY data into one Query with the Help of Append feature.
Select "CY" query from Queries Pane on left side and then Go to Home Tab → Append Queries → Append as New Queries.
In the Append queries window select "Advanced" and select "PY" then click on "Add" button and click on OK. A new query is created named "Append1". Change the name of the Query as "Sales Data".

Insert Year and Month columns

Select "Bill Date". Go to Add Column tab and click on Column from Examples → Select from selection.

A new column will appear. Type Year in the cell and select the "Year". In current scenario select "2020". Press Enter and click "OK"

Similarly Select Bill Date column. Go to Add Column tab and click on Column from Examples → Select from selection. A new column will appear. Type Month in the cell and select the "Month". In current scenario select "Month". Press Enter and click "OK"

Reorder Columns

Reorder columns and change the location where you want to place it. Select number of columns required for more than one → Press Ctrl and select columns → Right click → Move → select out of 4 options available. Another way to move is by selecting the column press left click and drag to location as required.

Remove Other Columns and Pivot

Right Click on Sales Data and click on Reference. Rename the New query as "Placewisesales"

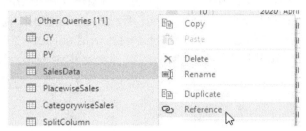

Go to Home Tab → Choose columns → Select Choose columns → Select Column heads Year, Month Name, Place, Taxable Value. In this way you can remove unwanted columns from the query.

Pivot Columns

Select Year column go to Transform tab and Select "Pivot Column"

A Pivot window will pop up from drop down select "Taxable Value" and click on "OK"

The Result of Pivot column is shown in image. First the years were in rows now after pivot the two years are shown in columns.

	A^B_C Place	A^B_C Month Name	1$^2_3$ 2020	1$^2_3$ 2019
1	AGRA	August	387903470	null
2	AGRA	July	387903470	null
3	AGRA	June	387903470	387650680
4	AHMEDABAD	August	903550	null
5	AHMEDABAD	July	903550	null
6	AHMEDABAD	June	903550	900540
7	AHMEDABAD	May	78355	-2855
8	ALIBAG	August	552575	null
9	ALIBAG	July	552575	null

Group Rows/Transpose Table/ Promote Headers

Right Click on Sales Data and click on Reference. Rename the New query as "Categorywisesales"

Go to Home Tab → Choose columns → Select Choose columns → Select Column heads Category and Taxable value.

Group By

Select text column Category and Go to Home Tab → Group By

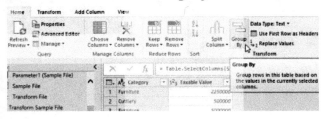

A new window will pop up. Below Operations select "Sum" in Column select "Taxable Value"
In New column name change it to "Sales". Click on OK

Result of Group by is it will summarize the values of each Category.

Transpose

Select the both the columns. Go to Transform Tab → Transpose.

The Data will be transposed in columns

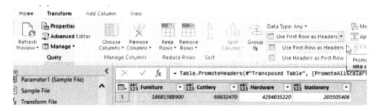

Promote Headers

Go to Home tab → Select Use first row as Headers → select use first row as headers.

Change Type

Select all the columns. Go to Home Tab → Data Type → Select Decimal Numbers.

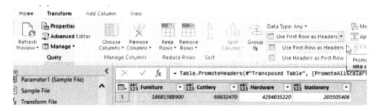

Split Column

Right Click on Sales Data and click on Reference. Rename the New query as "SplitColumn"

Go to Home Tab → Choose columns → Select Choose columns → Select Column heads Bill Date.

Select Bill Date and change type to Text.

Select Bill Date column and Right click and select "Split Column" and select by Dilimiter.

After selecting by Dilimiter a window will pop up. From drop down select custom then below

Put " – ". In Split by select each occurrence of the delimiter.

After splitting the date is separated in 3 columns

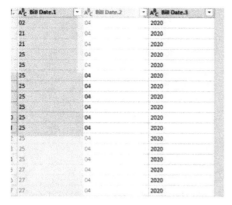

Bill Date.1	Bill Date.2	Bill Date.3
02	04	2020
21	04	2020
21	04	2020
25	04	2020
25	04	2020
25	04	2020
25	04	2020
25	04	2020
25	04	2020
25	04	2020
25	04	2020
25	04	2020
25	04	2020
25	04	2020
27	04	2020
27	04	2020
27	04	2020

Remove Duplicates

Right Click on Sales Data and click on Reference. Rename the New query as "Remove Duplicates"

Go to Home Tab → Choose columns → Select Choose columns → Select Column heads Party name and Sales person. Select both the columns go to Home tab Remove rows and select Remove duplicates. Another way is right click and select Remove Duplicates.

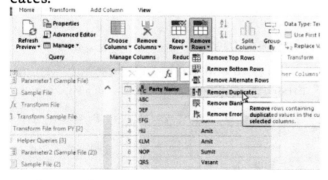

Replace Values

Right Click on Sales Data and click on Reference. Rename the New query as "Replace Values"

Select Unit column and Replace value window will pop up.

In Values to Find type "Nos" and in Replace with type "Units" and press OK.

Rename Column

Right Click on Sales Data and click on Reference. Rename the New query as "Rename column"

Go to Home Tab → Choose columns → Select Choose columns → Select Column heads Category, Description of goods and Taxable value. Double click on the column name and change the name of Taxable Value to "Sales"

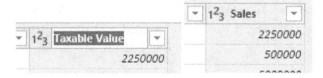

Transform Character in the Column

Right Click on Rename Column and click on Reference. Rename the New query as "Transformcharacter"

Select the Category column → Right click → Transform → Uppercase.

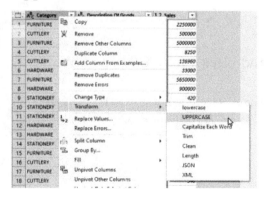

Transform a unstructured data into a Structured Data

As shown in the image the data provided is in unstructured format, Blank rows, Merged cells, Multiple columns, Formula errors not in a tabular format. With the help of Power Query we can clean and transform the Data and prepare a structured data.

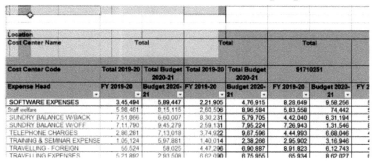

Go to Data Tab → New Query → From File → From Workbook → Locate the file and select the file and click on Import.

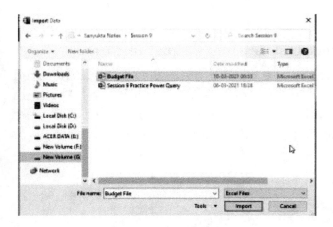

The Data will get imported in Power Query and can be seen in Power query editor as shown in the Image

Remove Top Rows

This feature removes the required number of top rows.

A new window will pop up. Input Number of rows to be removed

The result will be as shown in the image

Select all the data with Ctrl + A and Transpose the data from Transform tab → Transpose

Promote the Headers

Go to Home tab → Use first row as headers.

As you can see in 1st column there are null values in alternate rows. Cost center code needs to be populated in next row for

each instance. To do this use **Fill down Feature.**

Right click on the selected column → Fill → Down

Result will be as shown in the image.

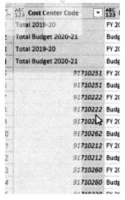

Remove Top 4 Rows. Home tab → Remove Rows → Top rows → and type number of rows required to be removed.

	ABC 123 Cost Center Code		ABC 123 Expense Head		ABC 123 ADVERTISIN
1	Total 2019-20		FY 2019-20		
2	Total Budget 2020-21		Budget 2020-21		
3	Total 2019-20		FY 2019-20		
4	Total Budget 2020-21		Budget 2020-21		
5			91710251	FY 2019-20	

Unpivot Other Columns

Select 1st 2 columns → Right Click → Unpivot other columns

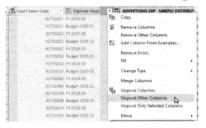

Result will be as shown in the Image

If any errors in any column. Select the column → Right Click → Replace Errors

A new window will pop up. Give required value. If Number column then number value. If Text then text value

If still Error remains then go to home tab → Remove Rows → Remove Errors

Import CSV Data

Go to Home Tab → New Query → From File → From CSV

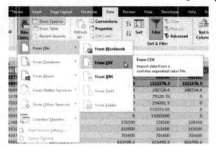

Select the CSV Fie and Import

A new window will pop up. Select the File origin, Delimiter and Data type Detection and then click on Load → Load to → Table.

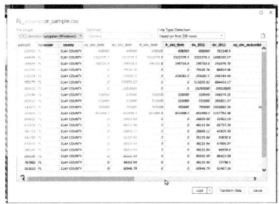

File Origin options. Select the relevant origin of CSV.

Select the Delimiter from the list

Select data type detection currently Based on first 200 rows is selected.

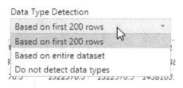

Import Text File

Go to Home Tab → New Query → From File → From Text

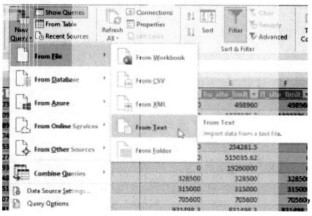

A new window will pop up. Select the File origin, Delimiter select "Tab" and Data type Detection and then click on Load → Load to → Table.

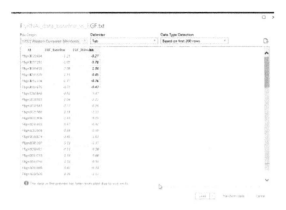

Import Data From Web

Data Tab → New Query → From Other Sources → From Web

Data From Web

https://en.wikipedia.org/wiki/
List_of_states_and_territories_of_the_United_States

Paste above link in Web browser and in power query URL. As shown in image

Copy the link and paste in the URL box and click Ok

A Web connector window will pop up. Select Anonymous and Click Ok

The available authentication methods for this connector are:
Anonymous: Select this authentication method if the web page doesn't require any credentials.

Windows: Select this authentication method if the web page requires your Windows credentials.

Basic: Select this authentication method if the web page requires a basic user name and password.

Organizational account: Select this authentication method if the web page requires organizational account credentials.

Select the States of the United states of America table and select Load to table.

Similarly Import Stock Market Data from Below link and follow same steps as given above and select "Table 0" and Load to table.

https://www.moneycontrol.com/stocks/marketinfo/marketcap.php?optex=BSE

Steps to Automate Sales Analysis Report with Excel Database. (Note to change the data source of base data check steps on last page of this note)
Data Given
1. Month Wise sales data 2020 & 2019 (Apr, May, Jun, July, Aug). Two folders PY and CY.
2. Master
    a. OverheadRatio

b. SP_Commission (Sales Person Commission)

c. Tax

Steps

1. Import Month wise sales data and append in one table in power query

2. Import Masters and merge with the appended table

Import Sales Data from Folder

Go to Data tab → New Query → From file → From Folder

After Clicking on from folder browse to the folder required to be imported. Select the CY and click on open.

In Combine window select Combine → Combine and load to. A new window will pop up → Select "only create connection" and untick on others and click "OK".

Similarly import "PY" data and import it to power query.

Import Master tables

Go to Data tab → New Query → From file → From workbook

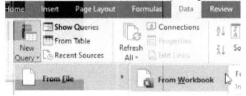

Select the master file and click on Import

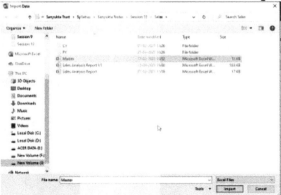

Select all the 3 Tables OverheadRatio, SP_Commission, Tax as shown in the image and click Load to and select "Only create connection"

The Data imported is stored in power query and can be seen in Workbook queries as shown in the image

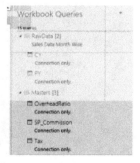

Create folders in workbook queries pane and organize the queries for better navigation and identification of Data.

Right click on "CY" → Move to Group → New Group → Name it as Raw Data .

Move the PY query to Raw Data folder
Right click on the "PY" → Move to Group → Raw Data.

Similarly Create Folder for Masters.
Right click on "CY" → Move to Group → New Group → Name it as
Masters.

Append "CY" and "PY" data.
Click on "CY" and go to Append Queries → Append Queries as

New

Name the new queries as "SalesCYPYBaseData"

SalesCYPYData

Right click on the SalesCYPYBaseData and select Reference and name it as"SalesCYPYData"

Merge the Masters in SalesCYPYData.
Overhead Ratio
Go to Merge Queries and → Select Merge Queries

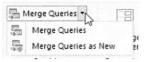

In Merge window Select Overhead Ratio table and select Category in both the data and click on OK

Expand the Column and select Overhead Ratio

SP Commission

In Merge window Select SP commission table and select Sales Person Name in both the data and click on OK

Expand the column and select Commission

Tax Master

In Merge window Select Tax table and select Description Of Goods in Sales Data and Goods in Tax in both the data and click on OK

Expand the column and select Tax

Add Column for Calculating Overhead Cost, Sales person commission and Tax Value columns

OH Cost Column

Go to Add Column tab → Select Custom Column

Name it as OH Cost and in formula window select Overhead %
then press "*" and then select Taxable value and click ok

Taxes Column

Go to Add Column tab → Select Custom Column
Name it as Taxes and in formula window select Tax.1 then press
"*" and then select Taxable value and click ok

Commission Column

We want commission in 0.2 format hence select the Commission column and go to Transform Tab → Select Standard → Select Divide and divide it by 100.

Go to Add Column tab → Select Custom Column
Name it as CommissionofSP and in formula window select
Commission then press " * " and then select Taxable value and
click ok

Profit Column

Go to Add Column tab → Select Custom Column
Name it as Profit and in formula window select Taxable value
then press minus and then select Cost press minus select OH
Cost press minus select Taxes press minus select commissionofSP and click ok

Insert Year Month name and Week Columns

Year

Select Bill Data column and Go to Add column → Column from examples → from selection

In new column type Year select 2020 and press enter and click on OK

Month Name

Select Bill Data column and Go to Add column → Column from examples → from selection

In new column type Month select Month and press enter and click on OK

Week

Select Bill Data column and Go to Add column → Column from examples → from selection

In new column type Week select week and press enter and click on OK

Change type

Select OH cost , Taxes, CommissionofSP & Profit and change the type to decimal numbers. Go to Home tab → Data type → Decimal Numbers

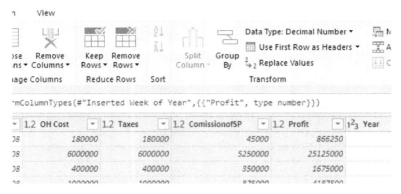

Go to Home Tab → Close and Load to → Load to Table.

Exception Report to find out incomplete masters

Create a Reference Query of SalesCYPYBase Data. Right click on the SalesCYPYBaseData and select Reference. Name the New Query as Exception for commission.

Merge SP commission with the data. Select Sales person name in both table and click OK.

Expand the Commission Column.

Go to Home tab → Choose columns. Select Sales Person name and commission Column

Select Both the columns and right click and select remove duplicates
Select Commission Column and Select "null"

You will get Sales person Name who's name is not there in the Commission master and which needs to be updated. In current scenario Varun and Durgesh name is not present in master and there commission needs to be updated.

	ABC Sales Person Name	123 Commission
1	Varun	null
2	Durgesh	null

Go to Home Tab → Close and Load to → Table and click OK
Open the Master file and add the name of Varun and Durgesh in the table of Commission and put commission

Sales Person Name	Commission
Joel	10
Priya	3
Naseer	7
Ganesh	2
Manish	9
Ramesh	10
Deepesh	9
Amit	7
Sumit	3
Rana	8
Sneha	10
Pravin	8
Sameer	2
Nitin	3
Shiv	6
Prakash	1
Vikas	10
Ajay	2
Jhon	5
Rahul	2
Jayant	1
Vasant	7
Pratik	4
Sumit	6
Varun	2
Durgesh	6

Save the Master file and close it

Go to Sales analysis Report → Data Tab → Refresh All

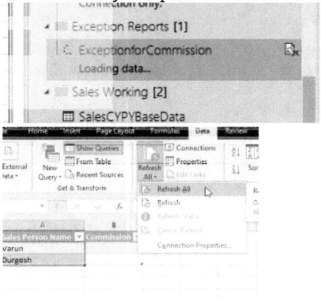

After Refresh the Master is updated and there are no more exceptions.

Change the Data Source Settings

GO to Data tab → New Query → Data source Settings

Change the Source of the Base data in below window. Select 1st link ends with CY → Click on Change source

Click on Browse and locate the folder where the data is stored

Select the CY folder and click on Open

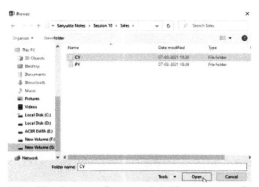

Similarly perform similar steps for "PY" and "Master" and then click on Close.

POWER PIVOT

Power Pivot

Power Pivot is a Powerful data analysis and data modeling tool in Excel.

Power Pivot is an Excel add-in you can use to perform powerful data analysis and create sophisticated data models. With Power Pivot, you can mash up large volumes of data from various sources, perform information analysis rapidly, and share insights easily.

In both Excel and in Power Pivot, you can create a Data Model, a collection of tables with relationships. The data model you see in a workbook in Excel is the same data model you see in the Power Pivot window. Any data you import into Excel is available in Power Pivot, and vise versa.

How the data is stored

The data that you work on in Excel and in the Power Pivot window is stored in an analytical database inside the Excel workbook, and a powerful local engine loads, queries, and updates the data in that database. Because the data is in Excel, it is immediately available to PivotTables, PivotCharts, Power View, and other features in Excel that you use to aggregate and interact with data. All data presentation and interactivity are provided by Excel; and the data and Excel presentation objects are contained within the same workbook file. Power Pivot supports files up to 2GB in size and enables you to work with up to 4GB of data in memory.

Saving to SharePoint

Workbooks that you modify with Power Pivot can be shared with others in all of the ways that you share other files. You get more benefits, though, by publishing your workbook to a SharePoint environment that has Excel Services enabled. On the SharePoint server, Excel Services processes and renders the data in a browser window where others can analyze the data.

On SharePoint, you can add Power Pivot for SharePoint to get additional collaboration and document management support, including Power Pivot Gallery, Power Pivot management dashboard in Central Administration, scheduled data refresh, and the ability to use a published workbook as an external data source from its location in SharePoint.

Power Pivot Installation

For All Pro versions MS Excel 2013 and above Go to Developer Tab → Com Add-ins → Select Microsoft Power Pivot for Excel → Click Ok → Power Pivot Tab is enabled as shown in Image.

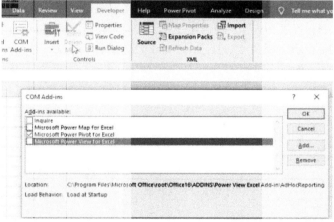

After enabling Power Pivot a New tab will appear

From the Power Pivot ribbon tab, select Manage from the Data Model section.

When you select Manage, the Power Pivot window appears, which is where you can view and manage the data model, add calculations, establish relationships, and see elements of your

Power Pivot data model. A data model is a collection of tables or other data, often with established relationships among them. The following image shows the Power Pivot window with a table displayed.

The Power Pivot window can also establish, and graphically represent, relationships between the data included in the model. By selecting the Diagram view icon from the bottom right side of the Power Pivot window, you can see the existing relationships in the Power Pivot data model. The following image shows the Power Pivot window in Diagram view.

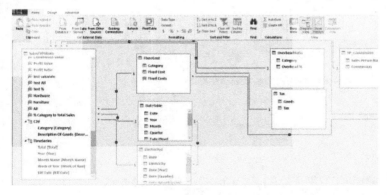

Load Data to Power Pivot and Create a Data Model

External Data other than Excel can be imported in Power Pivot window

There are Two ways to import data to Power Pivot

1. In Power Pivot Tab → Select the Table → Go to Add To Data Model

2. Right Click on SalesCYPYData click on LoadTo .. In Load to window click on Only Create Connection and Select Add this data to Data Model and click OK

In Power Pivot window under the measures sections type "SUM" formula

Syntax : SUM:=(ColumnName)

We can mention the tablename with the column name.

Formula - Sale:=SUM(SalesCYPYData[Taxable Value]). It summarizes the values in the column

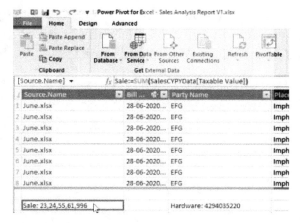

Similarly write "Sum" formula for Cost, OHCost, Tax Value, Commission Value

Formula for Cost → Costs:=SUM(SalesCYPYData[Cost])

Formula for OHCost → OHCost:=SUM(SalesCYPYData[OH Cost])

Formula for Tax Value → Tax Value:=SUM(SalesCYPYData[Taxes])

Formuma for Commission Value → Commission Value:=SUM(SalesCYPYData[ComissionofSP])

Derive Profit by deducting Costs from Sales Value

Profit Value:=[Sale]-[Costs]-[OHCost]-[Tax Value]-[Commission Value]

Profit Ratio

Profit Ratio:=[Profit Value]/[Sale]

Hierarchies in Power Pivot

One way you can modify a powerpivot data model is to add a hierarchy. For example if you have geographic data you can add a hierarchy that has a country at the top and drills down to region , state and city. It is a list of columns that rolls up to a single items in a power pivot. A Hierarchy appears as a single object in the Field List. It helps users to navigate and get deeper insights of data in a chart with drill up and down.

Go to Home → View → Diagram view

Select the SalesCYPYdata table. In that click on category column and right click and select create Hierarchy.

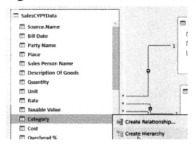

Name it as C2d.

C2d
Category (Category)
Description Of Goods (Descri...

Select Description of Goods right click and click on Add to hierarchy

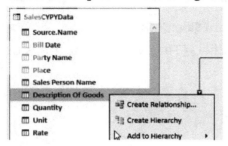

Below is the Hierarchy

C2d
Category (Category)
Description Of Goods (Descri...

Similarly Create TimeSeries hierarchy

Click on the Data View → In SalesCYPYData Add a "Total" Column.
="Total"

onofSP	Profit	Year	Month Name	Week of Year	Total	Calculat
14.4	170.4	2020	June	26	Total	
4278.3	60609.25	2020	June	26	Total	
3	42.5	2020	June	26	Total	

Click on Diagram view Go to SalesCYPYData table and create hierarchy of
Timeseries by Adding
Total, Year, Month, Week, Billdate

Close the Power Pivot window and save the file.

Go to Insert tab and Insert a Pivot. In Pivot table fields under SalesCYPY-data Select "C2d" and keep it in rows, select fx Sales in values.

Insert a chart. Keep cursor in pivot and press Alt+F1 or go to insert tab and insert a Bar chart.

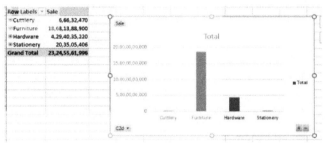

Double click on the Furniture Bar to drill down in data

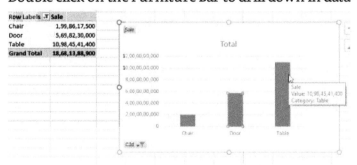

To go back again go to analyze tab → Drill up

Hierarchy helps to create interactive charts.

Relationship in Power Pivot

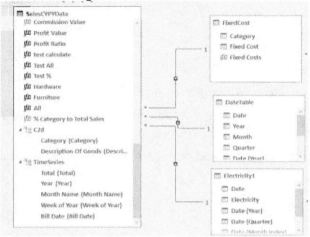

Working with multiple tables makes data more interesting and relevant to the PivotTables and reports that use that data. When you work with your data using the Power Pivot add-in, you can use Diagram View to create and manage the connections among the tables you imported. Creating table relationships requires that each table has a column that contains matching values.

Two separate data sets with a common column can be controlled and merged into one pivot with the help of Relationship feature.

In current example Sales Data is at detailed level, whereas Fixed cost is available at Category level.

Import 3 Masters from New Master Filles – Fixed Cost, Date Table, Electricity
Go to Data → New Query → From File → from workbook → New Master.
Select Multiple Items and select the three tables and click on create only connection and select "Add this data to data model" and click ok

Go to Power Pivot window click on Diagram view. There are total 4 tables.

Create a relationship with sales data and the three masters

Fixed Cost

Select Category in Sales Data → Left click and drag the mouse to Category in fixed cost and leave the mouse. Relationship is created

Date Table

Select Start of the Month in Sales Data → Left click and drag the mouse to Date in DateTable and leave the mouse. Relationship is created

Electricity

Select Start of the Month in Sales Data → Left click and drag the mouse to Date in Electricity and leave the mouse. Relationship is created

Insert a Sum formula in Fixed Cost Table in Power Pivot. Fixed Costs:=SUM(FixedCost[Fixed Cost])

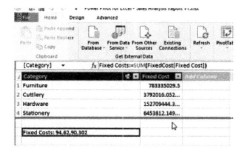

Go To SalesCYPYdata Table and insert Total Costs measure → Total Cost:=[Costs]+[Fixed Costs]

Close the Power Pivot Window. Go to Insert Tab and Insert Pivot table in a New worksheet **OR** from home tab insert Pivot Table.

In Pivot table fields From Fixed costs table select Category in Rows, Select Fixed Costs in Values, From SalesCYPYdata Select Costs and Total Costs in Values.

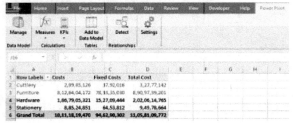

As seen in the image the pivot is prepared from two Tables SalesCYPYData and Fixed Cost

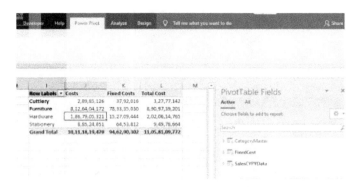

Calculate Function

Syntax = CALCULATE(<expression>, <filter1>, <filter2>...)
The expression that we put in the first parameter has to be evaluated to return the result (that is a value, not a table). For this reason, the expression is usually an aggregation function like SUM, MIN, MAX, COUNTROWS and so on.

This expression is evaluated in a context that is modified by the filters in the following parameters. A key point is that these filters can both enlarge and restrict the current context of evaluation.

Calculate with ALL function

ALL Function avoids all the filter selection of slicers.
Insert a measure of ALL as shown below. Select expression as sales and filter as ALL and in ALL select Category Column.

All:=CALCULATE([Sale],ALL(SalesCYPYData[Category]))

With the above measure the Sales total will remain same in the pivot with no effect of slicer filters

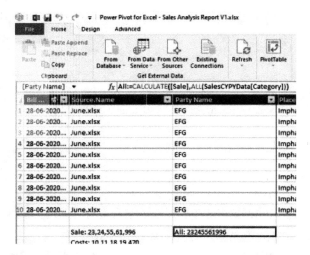

Close the power pivot window and Go to inset tab and insert a Pivot. Select Party Name, ALL, Sale and insert a slicer for Category and select any category. As you can see in the image the ALL column has not changed and its showing total whereas the sales is showing the filter selection of Furniture.

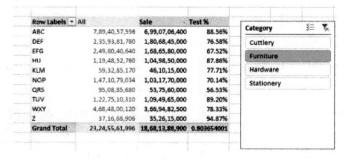

Calculate with Filter function

Go to Power Pivot window and in salescypydata → insert a measure for all four categories
Hardware, Stationery, Cuttlery and Funiture.

Syntax -- Stationery:=CALCULATE([Sale],FILTER(SalesCYPY-Data,SalesCYPYData[Category]="Stationery"))

In Calculate select Sale as expression and in filter insert Filter function and select the sales table and Category column and then type "=" and type "Stationery" and close the bracket. Similarly insert measure for other categories.

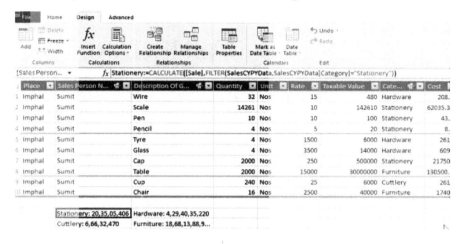

From the above measures we will get filtered data for all categories.

The Same measures can be used in Pivots.

Filter functions filters the data according to the criteria given. It's the same concept as we select a category from a filter. Filter function does the same function

CHARTS & DASHBOARD

CHARTS

It is a visual representation of data from a worksheet that can bring more understanding to the data than just looking at the numbers. A chart is a powerful tool that allows you to visually display data in a variety of different chart formats such as Bar, Column, Pie, Line, Area, Doughnut, Scatter, Surface, or Radar charts. With Excel, it is easy to create a chart.

Continuing with our previous practice files, we will create interactive charts from the data to make it more presentable and to get more insights.

Charts can be created from a structured data with proper heading and data supporting the same. We will create "Pivots" as our base data for charts.

Insert a sheet in Sales Analysis Report and name it as Pivot for Charts.

Timeseries sales Chart

Insert a Pivot and select Timeseries hierarchy in rows and Sales in values. Name the Chart in Analyze tab → Under Pivot table names as TimeseriesSales. And put a same heading above the pivot.

Now select the pivot and insert a bar chart.

There are 2 ways to insert a chart

1. Press Alt+F1
2. Inert Tab → Charts section

Select the 2D bar chart

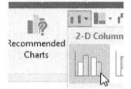

A chart will appear

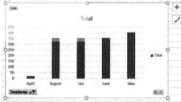

Remove the icons, gridlines and Legend

Keep Below selections for the chart. Give Title to chart as Time Series Sales and change the formatting of the title from Formatting tab

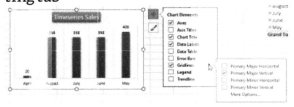

Right click on the chart and save it as Template so that we can use the same template for other charts.

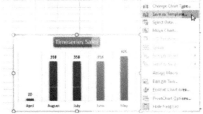

Save template as Sales analysis chart

If you click on the any of the Bar it will drill down from Year to Date and you can drill it up from Analyze tab → Drill up and Drill down button.

Category Wise Sales Chart

Insert Category wise sales Pivot

Select "C2d" hierarchy in rows and Sales in Values. Name the Pivot as Cat2GoodsSales. And give same as title.

Insert Chart in similar manner as above. Select the chart and Change the chart type from design tab

Select the template saved earlier.

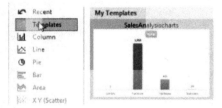

Change the title of the chart Category to Goods Sales and change the formatting and colour.

Category Pie Chart

Insert a pivot and select "Category" in rows and "Sales" in values. Name the pivot in Analyze tab as "CategoryPiechart".

Insert 2D Pie chart from Insert Tab under Chart section.

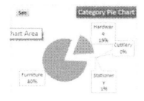

Click on the Plus sign and under Data labels select Data callout and then select outside End

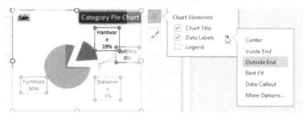

Right Click on the Chart and Select "Format Chart Area". Select the Pie → in Format data series pane under the Bar icon → Series options → Change the angle of first slice and increase the pie explosion as required.

Create Total Cost Measure in Power Pivot

Go to Power Pivot tab and click on Manage → SalesCYPYdata enter the below dax measure

Total Costs:=[Costs]+[OHCost]+[Tax Value]+[Commission Value]

Category Wise Profit Chart

Insert Pivot and Add Category in Rows, Sales, Total Cost and Profit Value in Values

Insert Bar chart from Insert Tab and change the chart type from design tab and select Template saved.

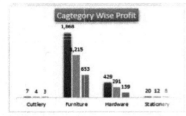

Sales Person wise Chart

Insert Pivot and select Sales person Name in Rows and Sales in Values and name the pivot as salespersonwisesales

Insert Bar Chart and change the chart type from design tab and select Template. Give it title.

Party wise Sales Chart

Insert Pivot and select Party Name in rows and Sales in Values. And name the pivot as partywisesales

Insert Bar chart and change the chart type from design tab and select the template. Give it title as Party wise sales

Create a new sheet and name it as " Sales Analysis" and move all the Charts to this sheet.

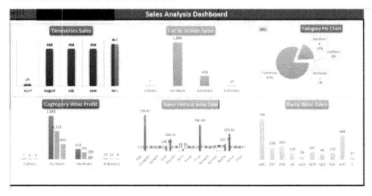

Arrange the Charts in this manner or in required manner you

desire.

Give a tittle as Sales Analysis Dashboard.

Dashboard

Let's Create an interactive Dashboard by adding Slicers

Click on any of the chart and go to Insert tab and click on slicers

Select Year, Month, Week, Party Name, Category, Place, Sales Person name.

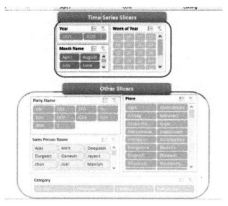

Right click on the slicers and click on Report connection and connect all the slicers with All the charts except the Category PIE chart.

Now the naming of Pivot tables will help you to select the pivots to connect with slicers.

Interactive Dashboard

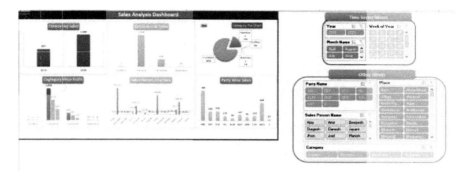

Automated Sales Analysis Dashboard

Store data in a Folder as shown in image. Update new data in the respective folder and files.

☐ CY
☐ PY
📊 Master
📊 New Masters
📊 Sales Analysis Report

When new data is updated in respective files save it and open the Sales analysis Report go to Data tab and click on Refresh All. Power query will update the data at back end and Power pivot data will also get updated.
Similarly all charts and slicers will get updated.

Change Path of Data
Click on New Query and Click on Data source setting

Select the data source one at a time click on change source and change the Path and browse it to required path and click ok. Repeat for all the sources and then click on close.

VBA Macro

VBA Macros use the Visual Basic Application in Excel to create custom user-generated functions and speed up manual tasks by creating automated processes. One of its main uses is to change and customize the user interface by creating personalized toolbars, menus, dialog boxes, and forms.

How to Use Excel VBA

Users cannot directly manipulate the main Excel software through VBA, they can, however, master the art of making macros to optimize their time in Excel. There are two ways to make Excel macros.

1. Macro Recorder
2. VBA Code

The first method is to use the Macro Recorder. After activating the recorder, Excel will record all the steps a user makes and save it as a "process" known as a macro. When the user ends the recorder, this macro is saved and can be assigned to a button that will run the exact same process again when clicked. This method is relatively simple and requires no inherent knowledge of the VBA code. This method will work for simple processes.

However, the downfall of this method is that it is not very customizable, and the macro will mimic the user's input exactly. By default, recorder macros also use absolute referencing instead of relative referencing.

The second and more powerful method of creating an Excel macro is to code one using VBA.

Where to Code Excel VBA?

To access the VBA window, press Alt + F11 within any Office program. When done properly, this will open a window with a file structure tree on the top left, properties on the bottom left, a debug pane at the bottom center and bottom right, and the coding section that takes up the majority of the screen in the center and top right. This may seem overwhelming at first, but in reality, it's simpler than it appears.

Most of the time, the user will be working in the coding section.

The file structure section is only used for creating a new macro file. The properties section in the bottom left will only be used for more advanced macros that use UserForms to create graphical interfaces for the macro.

The coding section is where most, if not all, the coding happens. The user will create, code, and save macros here. After the macro code is written and saved, it can then be attached to certain triggers in the Excel model. The macro can be activated at the push of a specific button on the worksheet, or when certain cells are modified, for example. The easiest way to implement a macro is to attach it to a button.

Let's Create first Macro by Record Macro

Open the Sales Analysis Report

1. RefreshData

Go to Developer Tab → Click on Record Macro

In Record Macro window, In Macro name type RefreshData. In store macro in select This Workbook. And click "OK".

In Data Tab → click on Refresh ALL

Once Refresh is done go to Developer Tab → Click on Stop Recording

Stop Recording

Now click on Visual Basic to open Visual basic editor. In the code window a Refresh Data code is created under Module 1.

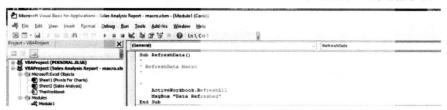

Now enter a new line of code after the RefreshALL

MsgBox "Data Refreshed"

This code will show a Message box after the code is run.

If the Project window is not visible click on View and click on Project Explorer and if code window is not visible click on Code.

2. ConvertoPPT

Go to Developer Tab → Click on Record Macro

Go to View tab and untick Gridlines, Formula Bar, Headings.

Go to Developer tab and click on Stop recording.

Click on Visual Basic to open VBA editor

In the code generated enter a new line after "Application.DisplayFormulaBar = False"

Application.CommandBars.ExecuteMso "HideRibbon"

This code will hide the ribbon.

Enter MsgBox code also to show a msgbox after the code is run.

MsgBox "Converted to PPT"

```
Sub ConverttoPPT()
'
' ConverttoPPT Macro
'

'
    ActiveWindow.DisplayGridlines = False
    ActiveWindow.DisplayHeadings = False
    Application.DisplayFormulaBar = False
    Application.CommandBars.ExecuteMso "HideRibbon"
    MsgBox "Converted to PPT"
End Sub
```

3. Convert to Normal

Go to Developer Tab → Click on Record Macro → Name It as Normal and click ok

Go to View Tab → and tick mark gridlines, formula bar and headings

Click on Stop recording. Go to Visual basic editor

In the Normal Code generated enter
Application.CommandBars.ExecuteMso "HideRibbon"

The above code will unhide the ribbon
Input Msgbox code in next line
 MsgBox "Converted to Normal"

4. Hide Sheets
Go to Developer Tab → Click on Record Macro → Name It as HideSheets

Right Click on Pivot for Charts and click on Hide

Click on Stop recording. Go to Visual basic editor and enter
Input Msgbox code in next line
MsgBox "Sheets Hidden"

5. Unhide sheets
Go to Developer Tab → Click on Record Macro → Name It as HideSheets

Right Click on Pivot for Charts and click on Hide

Click on Stop recording. Go to Visual basic editor and enter
Input Msgbox code in next line
MsgBox "Sheets Unhide"

Macro Enabled workbook
Go to File tab and click on Save As the Sales analysis report as Macro Enabled Workbook.

Macro will only work if it is saved in Macro enabled workbook i.e xlsm format.

Assign Macro

As we created the macros we can run the macro from VBA editor by keeping the cursor in required code and press "F5" or Play button

Another way to run is by creating a Shape in Excel and assigning the Macro to it.

In Excel create a shape. Go to Insert tab and Insert a Shape and name it as "Refresh"
Right click on the shape and Assign Macro, In Assign macro window select RefreshData and click OK

Similarly Create shapes for Convert to PPT, Convert to Normal , Hide Sheets and Unhide Sheets and assign the respective macros to respective shapes.

Now click on Convert To PPT Shape. You can see the macro will run and show a message Converted to PPT

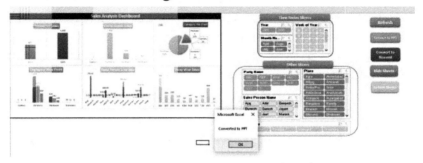

To go back to normal click on Convert to Normal

In this way you can click on the other buttons to use the macro created and automate your work instead of doing it manually.

POWER BI

Power BI is a collection of software services, apps, and connectors that work together to turn your unrelated sources of data into coherent, visually immersive, and interactive insights. Your data may be an Excel spreadsheet, or a collection of cloud-based and on-premises hybrid data warehouses. Power BI lets you easily connect to your data sources, visualize and discover what's important, and share that with anyone or everyone you want.

The parts of Power BI

Power BI consists of several elements that all work together.

- A Windows desktop application called Power BI Desktop.
- An online SaaS (Software as a Service) service called the Power BI service.
- Power BI mobile apps for Windows, iOS, and Android devices.
- Power BI Report Builder, for creating paginated reports to share in the Power BI service.
- Power BI Report Server, an on-premises report server where you can publish your Power BI reports, after creating them in Power BI Desktop.

Power BI Desktop

Power BI Desktop is a free application you install on your local computer that lets you connect to, transform, and visualize your data. With Power BI Desktop, you can connect to multiple different sources of data, and combine them (often called modeling) into a data model. This data model lets you build visuals, and collections of visuals you can share as reports, with other people inside your organization. Most users who work on business intelligence projects use Power BI Desktop to create reports, and then use the Power BI service to share their reports with others.

The most common uses for Power BI Desktop are as follows:
- Connect to data
- Transform and clean that data, to create a data model
- Create visuals, such as charts or graphs, that provide visual representations of the data
- Create reports that are collections of visuals, on one or more report pages
- Share reports with others by using the Power BI service

There are three views available in Power BI Desktop, which you select on the left side of the canvas. The views, shown in the order they appear, are as follows:

- Report: In this view, you create reports and visuals, where most of your creation time is spent.
- Data: In this view, you see the tables, measures, and other data used in the data model associated with your report, and transform the data for best use in the report's model.
- Model: In this view, you see and manage the relationships among tables in your data model.

The following image shows the three views, as displayed along the left side of the canvas:

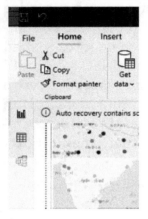

Base Data

Base data is Sales Data in excel for 2 years 2019 and 2020.

Connect to data

To get started with Power BI Desktop, the first step is to connect to data. There are many different data sources you can connect to from Power BI Desktop.

To connect to data:

1. From the Home ribbon, select Get Data > More.

The Get Data window appears, showing the many categories to which Power BI Desktop can connect.

Click on Excel and select the Sales Data → Sales Table

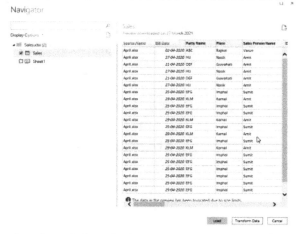

The data is loaded to power query and Power Pivot engine automatically. We don't need to load it to power pivot separately.

Below is the detailed explanation of Power BI desktop window.

Visuals window is were you plot the data in visualization and create a dashboard.

Filters pane – In this pane you can sort and filter selected data.

Visualization pane – Various pre configured visuals are stores which can be used to present data in charts form.

Fields – Data is stored which can be used to plot the data.

Ribbon – Used to navigate and used features of power Bi

Create Visuals

Click on the Report Icon on left corner.

Rename the Page 1 as Overview.

From Visualization pan click on Filled Map

Now Select Place from Fields Pane and place it in Location and Select Taxable value and place it in Legend. The data will get plotted on MAP in INDIA. Location will be picked up automatically.

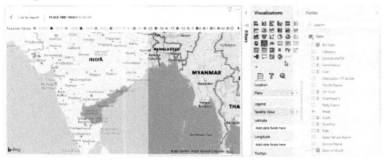

Click anywhere outside the Map chart and select Stacked chart

Select Party Name from fields pane and put it in Axis and Select Taxable Value and put it in Values

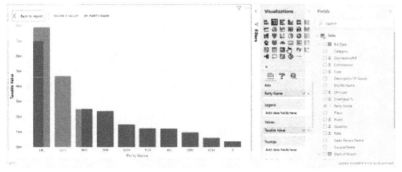

Click outside the chart anywhere and select Donut Chart

Select Category in Legend and Taxable value in Values.

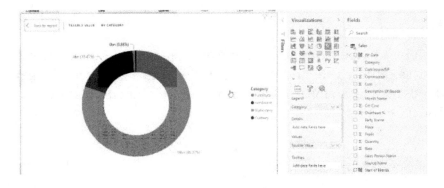

In this way you have created a your 1st visuals in Power BI Desktop

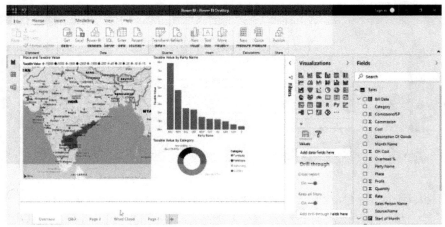

These Visuals are interactive and connected to each other. If you click on any of the chart other chart gets filtered automatically. This is one of the features of Power BI

Lets Select Furniture in Donut chart. As seen in the image other

2 charts got filtered for furniture selection and is showing data related to furniture category. To go back click again on furniture.

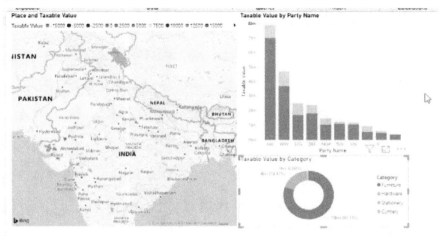

Create one more Page and name it as Q & A

Select the Q&A chart from visualization Pane.

This visual is a backed by AI (Artificial intelligence). You can as conversational questions related to the Data. For Example Type Sales person wise Taxable Value. It will plot a chart and show the same automatically.

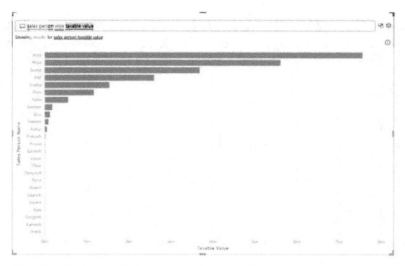

Similarly type Category wise Profit

In this way you can interact with data on the fly.

This is also one of the powerful features of Power BI

Get More Visuals

You can download more visual from Power BI Visuals Store.

Lets Download a visual named Word Cloud.

Create a fun visual from frequent text in your data

Word Cloud is a visual representation of word frequency and value. Use it to get instant insight into the most important terms in your data.

With the interactive experience of Word Cloud in Power BI, you no longer have to tediously dig through large volumes of text to find out which terms are prominent or prevalent. You can simply visualize them as Word Cloud and get the big picture instantly and user Power BI's interactivity to slice and dice further to uncover the themes behind the text content.

Download and save it in a folder.

In visualization pane click on the 3 dots prompting get more visuals

Select Import visual from file

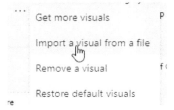

Browse the visual you downloaded and import it.

It will appear below the other visuals

Click on the Word cloud visual and select Place and put it category and select taxable value and put it in values. Place with highest value will be highlighted in bold and big sizes and place with lowest will be in lighter shade and small sizes as seen in image.

In this way you can get deeper insights of words in your data.

POWER BI DASHBOARD

Let's prepare a Dashboard in Power BI with the Sales Data table file in Excel.

Open Power BI Desktop and Import the Sales data file from Get Data and select the sales table and Load.

Name the Page in Power BI as Overview.

Download a New visual from Microsoft store of Power BI visuals. Timeline Slicer and download it.

https://appsource.microsoft.com/en-us/product/power-bi-visuals/WA104380786?src=office&tab=Overview

Import it into Power BI visuals

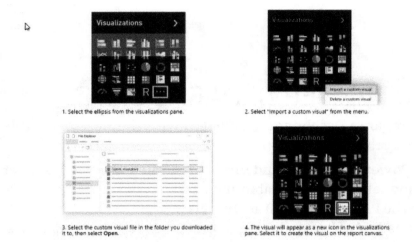

1. Select the ellipsis from the visualizations pane.

2. Select "Import a custom visual" from the menu.

3. Select the custom visual file in the folder you downloaded it to, then select Open.

4. The visual will appear as a new icon in the visualizations pane. Select it to create the visual on the report canvas.

Insert the Timeline Slicer and select Bill Date in time section of chart

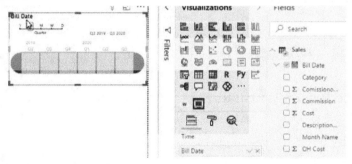

Insert Text box from Insert tab. Name it as Sales Analysis Dashboard

In visualization pane in background change the color. Select the Text change alignment to middle make it bold and change the color of text to White.

Insert stacked Donut chart. Put Category in Legend and Taxable value in Values.

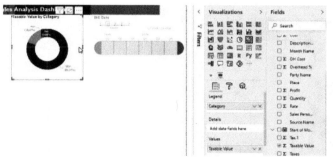

Click on format icon in visualization Pane

From this feature you can modify the chart as required.

Click on the Legend and select Off

Click on Detail Label and in label style select Category ,Percentage..

On Donut chart click on focus mode to enlarge the chart

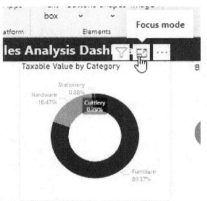

In Format tab → Title Text → Change the name to Category sales , Change background color and alignment. Switch on Border and shadow.

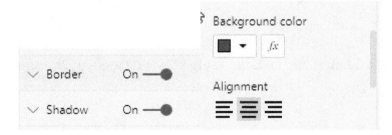

Final Chart will look as shown in image

Create Party Name sales, Sales person wise sales, Goods Sales and Place wise Map Charts

Click outside the chart and insert Stacked column chart

Party name Sales Chart -Select Party name and taxable value and format it. Chang the Title, give border and shadow, change data colours.

Sales person wise sales -Select Sales Person name and taxable value and format it. Chang the Title, give border and shadow, change data colours.

Goods Sales Chart -Select Description of Goods and taxable value and format it. Chang the Title, give border and shadow, change data colours.

Place Map Chart -Select Place and taxable value and format it. Chang the Title, give border and shadow.

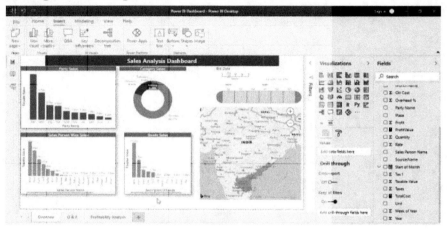

Click on Party Sales chart and click on the 3 dots → Show as Table

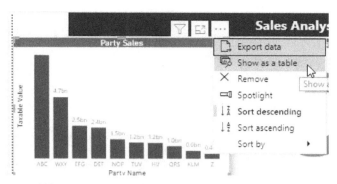

It will expand and show table and chart. To go back click on back to report.

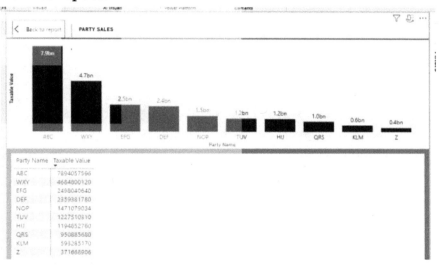

Insert New Page and Name it as Q & A
Insert the Q & A chart

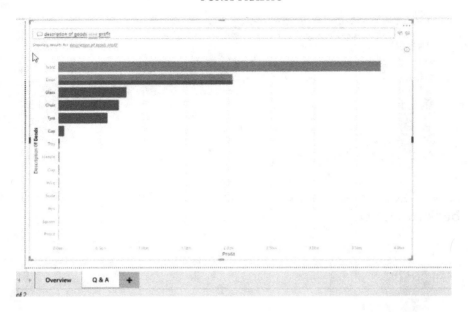

Insert new Page and Name it as Profitability Ananlysis
Click on Data

Now Insert a new measure from Table Tools and name it as
Total Cost

Insert Table chart and Select Category and Description Goods
Taxable value, Cost, OH Cost, CommissionofSP, Taxes
In formula bar Type sum and type Cost, type plus and type sum
and type OH Cost plus sum of CommissionofSP plus sum of

Taxes. In this way you have created a Total Cost measure.

```
1  TotalCost = SUM(Sales[Cost])+SUM(Sales[OH Cost])+SUM(Sales[ComissionofSP])+SUM(Sales[Taxes])
```

Select the Total Cost Measure to put it in table

Insert New Measure Name it as Profit Value and Type Sum Taxable value then type Minus and type

```
1  ProfitValue = SUM(Sales[Taxable Value])-[TotalCost]
```

Total Cost. Select the Profit Value Measure to put it in table.

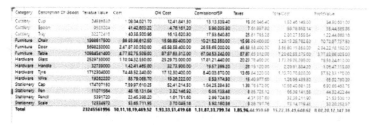

You can export the table in Excel format.

In this way we have created a Power BI dashboard.

This dashboard can be imported to Mobile phone format also. Go to Overview page and click on

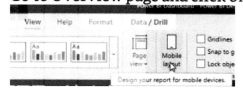

Select the required visuals from the visualization pane to be shown in mobile view.

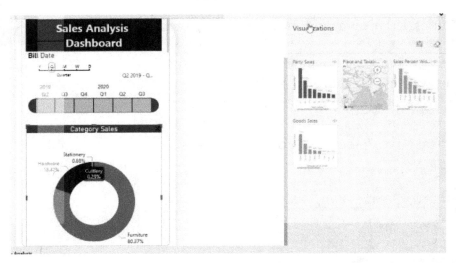

Sign in and publish this report to see in the mobile phone and if you want to share it with others with Microsoft ID

The Final Dashboard is as follows.

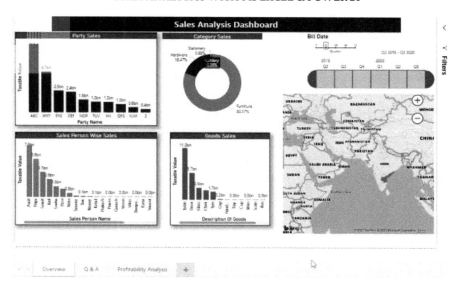

PRACTICE FILES LINK

https://drive.google.com/drive/
folders/10WsD3ETg4vqFxOMFy11iRIB4nce5Ar5j?usp=sharing

ACKNOWLEDGEMENT

I would like to thank my wife, Parents and my in laws for always supporting me and believing in me.
Also i would like to thank to all those with whom i have worked, for giving me an opportunity to get the rich experience i possess.
I would also like to thank the NGO for having faith in me
to teach an Indian Government recognized AIBTE course on Data Analytics with Excel and Power BI.

ABOUT THE AUTHOR

Punit Prabhu

Experienced Business Consultant with more than 10 years of experience in Data Analytics, Data mining, Digital Forensic and Cost Analysis, Cost control, Cost reduction. Also an MS Excel & Power BI enthusiast and address Excel related queries through WhatsApp, my blog and YouTube channel at a National and International Level. Catered to a diverse clientele across  industries. Also Taught a Government recognized course on Data Analytics with Excel and Power BI to students with various demographic in association with NGO.

BOOKS BY THIS AUTHOR

Automate Your Work With Microsoft Excel

Data Analytics With Excel

www.ingramcontent.com/pod-product-compliance
Lightning Source LLC
LaVergne TN
LVHW051336050326
832903LV00031B/3578